Purposeful Punctuation

Purposeful Punctuation

A Syntactic Guide to English Punctuation

By Dick Heaberlin

Writing Style 3

Orange House Books

San Marcos, Texas

For Additional Information Visit the Author's
Website at DickHeaberlinWrites.com

Copyright 2009 by Dick Heaberlin

ISBN 978-0-9794964-3-1

About This Book

My favorite recent American novel is Cormac McCarthy's *The Crossing*. In it, McCarthy doesn't punctuate conventionally. Whether or not it is a better novel because of its odd punctuation is debatable. There are certainly times when a reader is confused because of his nonstandard practice, but that is hardly the only cause of confusion in the work. I like it anyway.

I am not a purist about punctuation, but as an editor and writer I see many good reasons for knowing and using conventional punctuation. It is, first of all, an aid in clarity, showing proper relationship between the structures of our sentences, letting the reader know where one phrase, clause, or sentence ends and another begins.

Conventional punctuation is also a part of a long history of bookmaking, of typesetting, of the appearance of the work on the page. Some of the ways we punctuate seem counter-intuitive. For example, why do commas always go inside quotation marks? I've been taught that they do because early typesetters liked the way the page looked with them inside. Whatever the reason for the conventions we have, we have them. We have a social compact to be conventional when we are best served by doing so. At times, skillful and knowledgeable writers have chosen to go their own way and have punctuated unconventionally yet effectively in order to accomplish their purposes in particular sentences. Few are as unconventional as McCarthy.

This book is one of my guides to writing style. It should be fully understandable without a study of the other guides, but it will be much more easily understood if the reader has knowledge of the English sentence structures taught in Writing Style 1.

Contents

About This Book   5

Lesson 1
Punctuating the Basic English Sentence   7

Lesson 2
Punctuating Compounds   15

Lesson 3
Punctuating Series   25

Lesson 4
Punctuating Noun Modifiers   30

Lesson 5
Punctuating Other Parentheticals   38

Lesson 6
Punctuating Quotations   43

Lesson 7
Punctuating Exclamations   46

Lesson 8
The Wild Card — The Dash   47

Appendix 1
Answers and Explanations   60

Appendix 2
Practice Tests   79

Appendix 3
Answers to Practice Tests   87

Lesson 1

Punctuating the Basic English Sentence

Luckily, the basic English sentence needs little punctuation. When we line up our subject, verb, object, and adverbs in the usual order, no punctuation is needed. Here are some typical English sentences.

Bob Jones bought a computer yesterday at Best Buy.
Bob missed his class last night because of a late bus.

Bob works carefully when he is in the chemistry lab.

Adverbs such as *yesterday* and *carefully* are moveable. When we move the adverbs of these sentences in order to change the emphasis, we still need no punctuation most of the time.

Yesterday Bob Jones bought a computer at Best Buy.
Yesterday at Best Buy Bob Jones bought a computer.
Because of a late bus Bob missed his class last night.
Last night Bob missed his class because of a late bus.

Some writers put commas in some of these sentences to get special emphasis. They do it more frequently if the phrases are longer.

Yesterday, Bob Jones bought a computer at Best Buy.
Yesterday at Best Buy, Bob Jones bought a computer.
Because of a late bus, Bob missed his class last night
Last night, Bob missed his class because of a late bus.

Yet none is required by convention or for clarity.

Establishing Boundaries: Moving Verb-Modifying Clauses to the Front

Sometimes when we rearrange sentences, we have clarity problems. The following sentences are clear.

*My dogs were under my feet **while** I was cooking.*
*The horse fell down **while** I was riding.*

In these sentences, the boundary between *feet* and *I was cooking* and between *down* and *I was riding* is clearly marked by the subordinating conjunction *while*. There is no confusion and no necessity for marking the boundary between them with a mark of punctuation.

But if we move the verb-modifying clause to the front, we cause the reader to do a double-take. He will almost certainly misconstrue the meaning of the sentence and have to reread it.

While I was cooking my dogs were under my feet.
While I was riding the horse fell down.

This confusion can easily be cleared up by the placement of a comma where the verb-modifying clause joins the main clause. It is needed because there is no longer a subordinating conjunction to mark the boundary. It has been moved to the front.

While I was cooking, my dogs were under my feet.
While I was riding, the horse fell down.

Because of the confusion caused in some sentences by the lack of a comma here, it has become a convention of English punctuation to set off such initial verb-modifying clauses with a comma even when there would be no confusion without one. The following sentences are clear but not punctuated conventionally.

While Bill was working in the garage Sue was mowing the yard.
Although I got the job I still could not pay my bills.

Editors of almost all publications insist that the writers they publish follow the convention of placing a comma after these introductory clauses.

Any writer may learn to punctuate initial verb-modifying clauses conventionally by having a list of words like *while* and *although* ready to hand. I call this particular kind of subordinating conjunction a VMCI. This stands for Verb Modifying Clause Introducer. Here is a list of many of them.

Single Words: after, although, as, because, before, if, once, provided, providing, since, so, supposing, though, unless, until, when, where, whereas, while

Compounds: as often as, as if, as soon as, as though, at the place that, at the time that, during the time that, in case, in case that, in hopes that, in order that, even though, every time that, in the event that, now that, provided that, providing that, so that, supposing that,

A few of these structure words sometimes appear with a *that* and sometimes without one.

Provided that *I can get a ride, I will be at the party.*
Provided *I can get a ride, I will be at the party.*
So that *I could take a trip, I saved money.*
So *I could take a trip, I saved money.*

When using the two VMCIs of motive *in order that* and *so that*, writers may choose to omit *in order* and *so*.

In order that *he might win, he cheated.*
So that *he could win, he cheated.*

And they will get a rather formal variant which has the same meaning.

That *he might win, he cheated.*

There are a few horribly overlong VMCIs which I suggest that writers avoid. Here is a fairly complete list of the commonly used ones.

> along with the fact that, as a result of the fact that, because of the fact that, despite the fact that, due to the fact that, in contrast to the fact that, in spite of the fact that, owing to the fact that, plus the fact that, with the fact that, in addition to the fact that, within the period of time that

Editors must recognize them so that they can suggest shorter replacements. A comma will still be required after the initial clause should one of these ever be used. Notice this last sentence that I wrote.

A comma will still be required after the initial clause should one of these ever be used.

This is a case where a writer has a clause modifying a verb without a *VMCI*. Instead, we have the auxiliary verb moved to the front of the clause. If the clause is moved to the front, it is conventional to separate it from the following main clause with a comma.

Should one of these ever be used, a comma will still be required after the initial clause.

Exercise 1
Is a comma needed at the place or places underlined? Explain why or why not. Answers to this and all other exercises are in Appendix 1.
1. Bob finished his work in the lab _ early.

2. Bob may get home early _ if he can get to the bus on time.

3. If I see him _ I will give him your message.

4. Tim stayed at the lab late _ so that he could finish his work.

5. So that he could finish his work _ Tim stayed at the lab late.

6. As soon as Tim gets here _ I will give him your message.

7. When he got home _ I told him what you said.

8. In addition to the fact that he failed to put out the dog _ he didn't turn off the lights.

9. He will eat more ice cream _ although he said that he wouldn't.

10. Now that I am ready to go _ my ride still isn't here.

11. So I would be eligible to play baseball _ I studied every afternoon.

Establishing Boundaries: Putting Verb-modifying clauses after the Subject

So far, I have moved the verb-modifying clauses to the front, but the clauses can also be placed between the subject and verb. I don't usually recommend this placement if the clauses are exceptionally long. When verb-modifying clauses are after the subject, commas are conventionally placed on each side of them. This is one of the two primary functions of a comma, setting off one structure from another.

Bob, if he gets the message, will surely respond.
Tom, since he has been at home, has recovered quickly.

Exercise 2
Is a comma needed at the place or places underlined? Explain why or why not.

1. Hal _ when he gets here _ will tell you what happened.

2. Hal will tell you what happened _ if you ask him.

3. If you ask him _ Hal will tell you what happened.

4. As I was going into the building _ Hal was coming out.

5. Although I like Margie _ I don't believe that she can be trusted.

6. Trees _ when they are planted in the summer _ will need lots of water _ if it doesn't rain.

Verb-modifying Infinitive Phrases of Motive

Another structure which modifies verbs is the infinitive phrase of motive. These infinitive phrases serve the same purpose as the clauses introduced by *so that* and *in order that*.

*Bob saved money **so that** his son could go to college.*
***So that** his son could go to college, Bob saved money.*
*I saved money **so that** I could go to college.*
***So that** I could go to college, I saved money.*

*Bob saved money **in order for** his son **to** go to college.*
*Bob saved money **for** his son to go to college.*
*I saved money **in order** to go to college.*
*I saved money **to** go to college.*

The infinitive phrase of motive begins with *in order, for*, or *to*. When these phrases are moved to the front of the sentence or placed after the subject, they are punctuated like the comparable clauses.

Lesson 1   11

In order for his son *to go to college, Bob saved money.*
For his son *to go to college, Bob saved money.*
In order to go to college, I saved money.*
To go to college, I saved money.*

*Bob, **in order for** his son **to** go to college, saved money.*
*Bob, **for** his son **to** go to college, saved money.*
*I, **in order to** go to college, saved money.*
*I, **to** go to college, saved money.*

Exercise 3
Is a comma needed at the place or places underlined? Explain why or why not.

1. To get to Austin from here _ I sometimes take Post Road.

2. I should wash my hair more often _ so that it will look better _ when I go out on a date.

3. In order to make enough money to pay tuition _ he has to work at two jobs.

4. The school_ in order to attract more basketball fans_ is giving discounts on the tickets.

5. He went to the store _ to buy milk.

Sometimes the verb-modifying clause which has been moved to the front has another structure placed before it.

When *I get there, I will fix the leak.*
*He thinks that **when** I get there, I will fix the leak.*

I retained the comma because the relationship between the verb-modifying clause and the clause that follows has not changed.
It is possible to leave out the *that* in this sentence, but it is unwise to do so because doing so causes confusion about which verb the *when* clause is modifying.

*He thinks **when** I get there, I will fix the leak.*

Purposeful Punctuation

Sometimes a careless writer will put the *that* in the wrong place.

He thinks when I get there that I will fix the leak.

I have seen still other writers mistakenly put two *thats* in and leave out the comma.

He thinks that when I get there that I will fix the leak.

Exercise 4
Is a comma needed at the place or places underlined? Explain why or why not.

1. He said that when he quits working at the grocery store _ he will take a vacation.

2. I hope _ you remember _ where you put the tools.

3. In order to speak proper French _ I had to learn that if the verb was in the future tense _ I should join the whole infinitive with the future endings.

4. I know that when Bob is playing _ every game leads to an argument.

5. He suspects that I will win the match _ if he serves poorly.

6. He thinks that if I whisper _ I am lying.

7. I know that Bob Jones _ when he is serving well _ can beat me.

8. I think that he will be back later_ although he said that he wouldn't.

Occasionally an initial adverbial prepositional phrase can cause difficulty in comprehension for a reader. Notice what happens when the following prepositional phrase is shifted to the front and no comma follows.

*The barn looked bad **in spite of** his cleaning.*

In spite of *his cleaning the barn looked bad.*

This last sentence must have a comma in order to make the sentence clear.

In spite of *his cleaning, the barn looked bad.*

In spite of the poor clarity in that sentence there is no consistency of agreement about placing commas after opening prepositional phrases. I have a choice. I can punctuate my last sentence as I did, or I can punctuate it with a comma.

In spite of *the poor clarity in that sentence, there is no consistency of agreement about placing commas after opening prepositional phrases.*

Many handbooks says that commas should be placed after longer introductory prepositional phrases, but I do not find that good writers follow this practice with any consistency.

Here is a list of common prepositions:

Single Word: aboard, about, above, across, after, against, along, amid, among, around, at, barring, before, behind, below, beneath, beside, besides, between, beyond, by, concerning, despite, down, during, except, excepting, for, from, in, inside, instead, into, like, near, of, off, on, outside, over, past, plus, regarding, respecting, save, saving only, through, throughout, till, to, toward, towards, until, up, upon, with, within, without

Compounds: à la, along with ,as a result of, aside from, because of, by dint of, by means of, by the use of, by way of, contrary to, due to, for the sake of, in addition to, in advance of, in case of, in conjunction with, in consideration of, in contrast to, in hope of, in hopes of, in lieu of, in place of, in reference to, in regard to, in spite of, in the direction of, in the event of, in the fashion of, in the manner of, in the middle of, in the style of, instead of, on account of, on behalf of, out of, outside of, owing to, through the use of, together with, with respect to, with the exception of

The lists I have provided in this chapter are of great importance to any writer or editor hoping to recognize the structures modifying verbs so that they can punctuate the basic sentence clearly and conventionally.

Lesson 2

Punctuating Compounds

Like the basic sentence, compounds need little punctuation. In fact, one of the most common violations of the conventions of punctuation is to place commas where they are not needed. Doing so rarely causes a misunderstanding by the reader, but putting a comma where it is not needed may unnecessarily slow down the reader and lead to a rather plodding style.

We use the coordinating conjunctions *and* and *or* to compound the parts of basic sentences.

> *Bill **and** Tom went to the grocery store.*
> *Bill wrote a novel **and** published it last year.*
> *Tom is sleepy **and** tired every day after work.*
> *Bill eats apples **and** oranges.*
> *Bill works carefully **and** methodically.*
> *Bill works with care **and** with enthusiasm.*

In my many years of teaching writing and editing, I have rarely seen such sentences mispunctuated. Few writers feel a need to place commas in them. But when they make longer compounds and when they think there is time for a breath, they will put commas in even though it is unconventional to do so. Here are examples of compound phrases which are mispunctuated.

> *He wanted to live near the ocean in a town which had great sandy beaches, and in a house with great big windows to provide him a view of that beach.*

> *He expected to go into business with his father, and thought he would make as much money as his father had.*

> *He wanted to live near the ocean in a town which had great sandy beaches, and wanted to go out onto the beach to look for shells.*

I have frequently seen sentences like these punctuated unconventionally. The writer seems to think because the compounded structures are long that a comma is needed to indicate a break or a place to breathe. Or maybe the writers are mispunctuating because they are confusing these long phrases with independent clauses. Independent clauses are separated by a comma and a coordinating conjunction. We need to consider why the comma between independent clauses is needed. Look at the following sentence and consider why it might confuse you.

Bill looked for Helen and Sue searched throughout the house for Joe.

At first, typical readers will think Bill is looking for both Helen and Sue. They will think that *Helen* and *Sue* are both objects of the preposition *for*. They will make that mistake because there is no comma after *Helen*. Only the verb *searched* shows them that they have misread the sentence. The presence of the comma in the following sentence prevents the misreading.

Bill looked for Helen, and Sue searched throughout the house for Joe.

So two things are being done here. The *and* is saying that one independent clause is added to another, and the comma is saying that there is a separation between the first noun and the second. Commas are used to join and to separate. Our task as writers is to know which job is being done when.

The coordinating conjunction *or* is like *and* because it connects parts of sentences. Notice these two sentences.

Bill will spend the summer with his parents in the south of France near Arles, or work with his older brother on a ranch in West Texas.

Sue will give the award to her father or her mother will give it to him.

One of these doesn't need the comma. The other does.

Bill will spend the summer with his parents in the south of France near Arles or work with his older brother on a ranch in West Texas.

Sue will give the award to her father, or her mother will give it to him.

Connecting some independent clauses with coordinating conjunctions and no comma will not lead to confusion, but because of the possibility of error in some, it is the convention to punctuate compounds of independent clauses with both a comma and the coordinating conjunction. Here are two that are punctuated unconventionally. They are not in the least confusing.

Bill is going to the movie and Tom is staying in the dorm.
Bill will invite Sue to the dance or he will go alone.

The two sentences should by convention have commas before the coordinating conjunctions.

Bill is going to the movie, and Tom is staying in the dorm.
Bill will invite Sue to the dance, or he will go alone.

When independent clauses are very short, many writers do not follow the convention of placing a comma before the *and* and *or*.

Bill is going and Tom is staying.

Other writers use commas even in these sentences, not knowing when a sentence is short enough. They figure it is better to be safe than sorry. Even short sentences can be confusing when the comma is omitted.

Bill likes Helen and Sue likes Tom.

For the exercises in this book, I prefer that you use a comma with the coordinating conjunction to separate independent clauses however short they may be.

Exercise 1
Is a comma needed at the place or places underlined? Explain why or why not.
1. *Bob has been visiting his sister in Terre Haute _ and plans to return by the beginning of September.*

2. *Jim wants to date Mary _ and Jill wants to date Jim.*

3. *I went to the movie to see a horror picture _ and I wasn't scared at all.*

4. *The relief pitcher entered the game in the ninth inning _ and picked up a save.*

5. *Sue took a class that required her to get up at six _ and one that kept her at school until eleven.*

6. *I hope that Bill will remember his old friends when he invites people to his party _ and I hope he invites some new friends.*

7. *Bob stopped playing the guitar _ and began playing the banjo.*

8. Bob can now play a banjo _ and a guitar well _ and he will start work on a cello soon.

The compounds we have been working on so far have been compounds of common nouns and pronouns, of adjectives in form, and of common adverbs and prepositional phrases. Now we will look at compounds of certain dependent clauses, some of which are confused with independent clauses, and the confusion leads to errors in punctuation. For example, we may have two *that* clauses.

*I know **that** he likes San Marcos and **that** his mother wants him to stay here.*

No commas are needed because they are obviously not independent clauses. But if we omit one or both *that*s, then the dependent nature of the compound seems less obvious, and many writers will punctuate it in a way to hide the dependent structure. This is inappropriate punctuation.

*I know **that** he likes San Marcos, and his mother wants him to stay here.*

I know he likes San Marcos, and his mother wants him to stay here.

There are several other dependent clauses and phrases that are sometimes punctuated as if they were independent. Here are examples of these unconventional punctuations.

I know what he wants to give his mother for Christmas, and what he can afford to give her.

He likes buying her presents when he has the money, and giving them to her on Christmas eve.

The man she married likes to surprise her at Christmas, and to give her a ring with a large stone .

Exercise 2
Is a comma needed at the place or places underlined? Explain why or why not.
1. When Bob came home _ and said that he would take out the garbage _ and he liked doing it _ everyone was surprised.

2. When Bob arrived early _ and when he started right to work _ everyone was surprised.

3. I am sure that he wanted us to stay at home if it rained _ and that we were right to do it.

4. I talked to him even though I didn't like him_ and even though he was rude to me.

5. Bob knows how to repair a car with a bad muffler _ and how to do it with used parts.

6. She likes to write a blog _ and read comments about her ideas.

7. Some people have too much time _ and too much money _ and they often try to find ways to keep from being bored.

8. I suspect she likes him _ and they will get married.

9. She likes him _ and they will get married.

10. I figured they would stop trying to get along _ and decide to separate.

In addition to the coordinating conjunctions *and* and *or* that separate dependent and independent clauses, there are coordinating conjunctions whose main function is to join independent clauses. They are *but, yet, so,* and *for*. Each of these has other functions. Before I take up these conjunctions individually, here are some examples of them in their usual function of joining independent clauses. These are not, strictly speaking, compounds like those formed with *and* and *or*, but grammarians call them compound sentences.

He tried hard, but he failed.
He tried hard, yet he failed.
He worked hard, so he succeeded.
He succeeded, for he worked hard.

The word *but* is also used to compound parts of sentences. Commonly it suggests contrast.

He tried hard but failed.
He was tired but still eager.
He worked with care but without a plan.

Yet, in addition to being a coordinating conjunction of contrast, can be an adverb of time. Here it is in both of these functions.

He will fail, yet he has not failed yet.

So, in addition to being a coordinating conjunction of cause, has several other functions. It modifies adjectives and adverbs and often does so in combination with a *that* clause.

He is so tall that he can touch the ceiling.

In this use there is no need for punctuation even if the *that* is omitted.

He is so tall he can touch the ceiling.

As we saw in Lesson 1, *so that*, the VMCI of motive, can be written without the *that*. Then, it may be confused with the coordinating conjunction and lead to unconventional punctuation. Which of the *sos* in the next two examples is the coordinating conjunction and which the VMCI?

He saved money so he could go to Rome.
He saved money for a vacation so he took one.

Which one needs the comma? Which doesn't? The first doesn't need one. Here is the conventional punctuation.

He saved money so he could go to Rome.
He saved money for a vacation, so he took one.

The first sentence can be revised by moving the clause modifying the verb to the front. In the second, the clause can't be moved.

So he could go to Rome, he saved money.
He saved money for a vacation, so he took one.

The *so* in the first can have a *that* added to it. The second can't. The coordinating conjunction of cause in the second can be paraphrased with *therefore*.

For, in addition to being a coordinating conjunction of cause, can be a preposition.

*He saved money **for** a vacation.*

I have seen writers making punctuation errors by confusing the preposition *for* with the coordinating conjunction *for*. Which one of these needs a comma to show the structure properly?

*He was arrested **for** his burglary of a jewelry store.*
*He was arrested **for** he stole jewels.*

The first sentence has the preposition, the second the conjunction. So they should be punctuated like these.

He was arrested for his burglary of a jewelry store.
He was arrested, for he stole jewels.

Notice that only in the first can we move the construction headed by *for* to the front.

For his burglary of a jewelry store, he was arrested

Exercise 3
Is a comma needed at the place or places underlined? Explain why or why not.
1. *Now that he has been working late _ he is _ so tired _ he can hardly crawl into bed.*

2. *He has been working late _ so he is not only tired _ but sleepy.*

3. *Because of his affection for Marie _ and because of his dislike of her*

mother _ Bob comes to see Marie _ but avoids her mother _ if it is possible.

4. Tim completed his degree in three years _ but he wishes he had not hurried _ for he fears _ he learned less than he might have.

5. Joe worked long hours _ for poor wages _ for years _ for he needed the money _ for his mother's hospital bills.

6. I haven't seen him yet _ but I heard Bill moved back into town _ and I heard he was looking for me.

7. Either Bob _ or Tom will attend graduation _ or regret it.

8. Many of my friends are friends of Bill _ and will want to see him when they have the opportunity.

One compound of parts of a sentence is punctuated differently from others — compound adjectives. We can replace the *and* with a comma.

The tall and skinny cowboy rode the rough string.
The tall, skinny cowboy rode the rough string.

Notice that this comma replaces the *and* which joins the two adjectives, so its function is not to separate, like most of the commas so far, but to join.

Comma Splices and Run-on Sentences

I wrote earlier about the error of leaving out commas in sentences like these.

Bill looked for Helen and Sue searched throughout the house for Joe.
Bill is going to the movie and Tom is staying in the dorm.

There is another kind of punctuation error that is possible for such sentences. That is leaving out the coordinating conjunction and just having a comma.

Bill looked for Helen, Sue searched throughout the house for Joe.

Bill is going to the movie, Tom is staying in the dorm.

This mistake is called a comma splice. This is considered a serious error by teachers of composition. Some student go further in not marking the boundary between independent clauses. They leave out the comma, too.

Bill looked for Helen Sue searched throughout the house for Joe.
Bill is going to the movie Tom is staying in the dorm.

Composition teachers call these run-on or fused sentences. Many students mistakenly think that a run-on sentence is a long, unwieldy sentence, but that is not what the phrase means. An extremely short sentence can be a run-on.

Bill quit his boss was glad.

This failure to punctuate appropriately confuses readers and probably causes them to quit reading — the ultimate failure to communicate.

Some composition teachers believe that the way to correct the run-on sentence is to place a semicolon between the two independent clauses. I don't recommend this except in special cases, mainly when the structure of each independent clause is similar.

He feared nothing; she feared everything.
Baseball is interesting; golf is boring.

I don't recommend using the semicolon because almost no writers I read punctuate that way. It's not the normal way of making this connection. In the following exercises, correct these mistakes by using a comma and coordinating conjunction or by placing a period between the clauses and capitalizing the first word of the second clause.

Bill quit, and his boss was glad.
Bill quit. His boss was glad.

Exercise 4
Punctuate the following sentences conventionally. Some may require you to make two sentences or add a coordinating conjunction. You may write in any *that*s which are needed to make the sentences clearer. Some sentences may require no commas.

1. Bill works on Saturday from noon to midnight but he still doesn't make much money.

2. Though Bill works he never seems to get ahead.

3. Enthusiastic healthy employees are very important to a company they should be paid a decent wage.

4. Bob's friend wants him to stop writing bad checks he says that Bob is sure to be caught soon.

5. Bill quit buying trashy novels he didn't quit reading them now he goes to the library.

6. Bill and Mary have problems I think they need to go to a counselor.

7. I quit my job so now I can't pay my bills.

8. I quit my job so I would have more time to study.

9. Bob was arrested for he passed a bad check.

10. Bob was arrested for passing a bad check.

Lesson 3

Punctuating Series

In addition to making compounds of the basic parts of a sentence we can also make a series out of them by putting *and* between each item in the series.

I talked to Bill and Bob and Tom about playing baseball with me.

In this case no comma is needed. This is not considered an error, but it is not the usual way to make a series. You remember how we used a comma in the adjective compound to replace an *and*.

The tall and skinny cowboy rode the rough string.
The tall, skinny cowboy rode the rough string.

We employ the same technique usually in punctuating series of parts of sentences. We replace the *and* between Bill and Bob with a comma.

I talked to Bill, Bob and Tom about playing baseball with me.

The authors of many newspaper style manuals punctuate a series in this manner — without a comma before the *and* that precedes the last item in the series. The more common practice is to put a comma before the *and* or *or*. In this guidebook, I will be following the practice of placing the comma there.

I talked to Bill, Bob, and Tom about playing baseball with me.

When the series comes at the end of the sentence, some writers will drop the *and* because the period will tell readers that the series is complete.

She liked pears, oranges, apples.

Sometime writers also will write the wordier *and* series if they think it accomplishes their purposes better.

She washed the dishes and put away the clothes and mopped the kitchen and bathed the kids. What a day!

The *ands* here do a better job of suggesting how much she has done. This practice should not be used too often because it may draw readers' attention away from the meaning of the sentence onto the unusual punctuation. Punctuating a series with all *ands* is not considered a violation of punctuation.

Exercise 1

Is a comma needed at the place or places underlined? Explain why or why not. Some sentences may not need to be changed.

1. I went to the store for milk, eggs _ and bread.

2. I worked at Luby's _ at Red Lobster _ and at Sirloin Stockade.

3. She graduated in three years _ and started to graduate school early.

4. She said that she liked baseball _ football _ and basketball _ but she said that she didn't like going to the games _ like watching them on TV _ or like hearing her boyfriend talk about them all the time.

5. The silly _ infantile _ and nauseating teenager made a scene in the cafeteria.

6. He said I bought a bike a car _ and a golf cart _ yet I didn't buy any of those. I bought a fishing rod _ a reel _ a fishing license.

More complex sentence parts can be used in series, also. Here is an example of a series of dependent nominal clauses.

I know that I will complete the novel, that it will be published, and that I will be famous.

Notice what happens when I drop out the second and third *that*. This is a fairly common practice of writers seeking to be more economical.

I know that I will complete the novel, it will be published, and I will be famous.

Now it looks as if I have a comma splice between *novel* and *it*. I don't. This is still a series of noun clauses. It looks even more difficult to punctuate when I remove the other *that*.

26 Purposeful Punctuation

I know I will complete the novel, it will be published, and I will be famous.

The sentence still contains a series of dependent clauses and is punctuated conventionally.

Here is another example of a fairly complicated series. This time it is series of clauses modifying a verb.

We won't leave until Bob puts the dog out, until Jim washes the dishes, and until Joe makes the bed.

Once again, some writers will omit the second and third VMCI.

We won't leave until Bob puts the dog out, Jim washes the dishes, and Joe makes the bed.

And again it looks as if there is a comma splice between *out* and *Jim*. But there isn't because these are not independent clauses.

Exercise 2

Is a comma needed at the place or places underlined? Explain why or why not.

1. I talked about going to summer school _ or staying home.

2. Bob likes reading _ watching TV _ and listening to music.

3. I hate for my roommate to lie around goofing off _ to leave the dishes in the sink _ and to play his music too loud.

4. He said _ he knew when _ where _ and how to buy the best horses at the best prices.

5. I hope that my son stays in school _ my daughter makes good grades _ and my dog does not go off hunting porcupines.

6. I know that when my dachshunds stay home _ they don't get their faces full of porcupine quills _ don't get covered with skunk musk _ and don't get sore paws from digging.

7. He told me what he had done _ what he would do _ what he wouldn't do.

8. Bob walked _ and talked _ and acted like a child.

9. I can play basketball today _ if I don't have to keep my grandkids _ if I can finish my grading _ and if my wife doesn't find a job for me.

10. He drives home from Austin _ goes by the grocery store _ and stops at the coffee shop.

    I have talked about confusing a series of dependent clauses with one of independent clauses. If we have three independent clauses, we may wish to write them as separate sentences and still put an *and* before the last one to signal an end.

    I washed the dishes carefully. I rinsed them. And I set them out to dry.

This series of three actions, since we have the same agent, could be written as a series of verb phrases.

    I washed the dishes carefully, rinsed them, and set them out to dry.

But how do I handle the series of actions if I keep all of the *I*s. I could use the conventional but unusual practice of putting *and*s between all three.

    I washed the dishes, and I rinsed them, and I set them out to dry.

Here is where most of us teachers of writing employ the semicolon.

    I washed the dishes; I rinsed them, and I set them out to dry.

This way we don't have a comma splice. But I am increasingly seeing skillful professional writers using a comma in sentences such as this. This usage appears in carefully edited textbooks and journal articles.

    I washed the dishes, I rinsed them, and I set them out to dry.

    For years, while editing, I have avoided comma splices like this by replacing the first comma with a semicolon. In doing the exercises, follow that practice, too.

Exercise 3
Punctuate the following sentences. Add an *and* or *or* if you need one. You may also want to add a *that* or two. You may make new sentences if you wish. Some sentences may not need to be changed.

1. Bob finished washing his car he turned off the water put the chamois and sponges away and put the car back in the garage.

2. Bob has finished washing his car he turned off the water he put the chamois and sponges away and he put the car back in the garage.

3. The team played best after they practiced hard after they ate a good meal and after they got a good night sleep.

4. He couldn't remember where they went what they bought or when they left.

Some writers think that just because they have a series, they need to use a colon. Here are examples of this mistake.

I like: swimming, skiing, tennis, and basketball.
He invited: Mary, Tim, Juan, and Yvonne.

Writers may have exceedingly long series and the rule for punctuating the clauses will remain the same.

He invited Mary, Julia, Tom, Tim, Juan, and Yvonne.

Lesson 3   29

Lesson 4

Punctuating Noun Modifiers

Some modifiers of nouns serve the purpose of limiting or restricting the meaning of the noun. Readers are better able to identify the noun because of the modifiers.

*We gave the baseball to the **big** man.*
*We gave the baseball to the man **on the right**.*
*We gave the baseball to the man **with the red cap**.*
*We gave the baseball to the man **who was wearing a red cap**.*
*We gave the baseball to the man **wearing a red cap**.*
*We gave the baseball to the man **who was chosen captain**.*
*We gave the baseball to the man **chosen captain**.*
*I know the man **to give the baseball to**.*
*We gave the baseball to the **big** man **on the right with the red cap**.*
*The man **to give the baseball to** is the **big** man **on the right with the red cap**.*

All of these words, phrases, or clauses in these examples are restricting the meaning of man—limiting or qualifying the noun so that the reader can identify which man is being identified by the writer. When the modifying word or phrase is used to restrict the meaning, no comma is used after the noun.

Some writers try to punctuate by noticing when they would breathe in reading a sentence aloud. This sometimes works, but in punctuating restrictive clauses it can lead to difficulty, particularly when the modifying phrase or clause is modifying a subject of the sentence and the structure is quite long. Notice this improperly punctuated sentence.

The students who tried to enter the contest at the last minute without having previously contacted the administrators of the contest or even their teachers, were ruled ineligible.

Anyone reading this aloud would probably need to breathe before the *were*, but the pause or breath there is meaningless as far as punctuation is concerned. That there is no pause or breath between *students* and *who* is quite significant. The lack of one indicates that the following structure is restricting the meaning of the noun that it modifies and that no comma is needed.

Another general rule to keep in mind is that the subject of a sentence is not separated from its verb by a single comma.

Parenthetical Noun Modifiers.

For noun modifiers that are not restricting meaning, the breath or pause after the noun is of great significance. If there is a breath, at least a comma is needed to show that what follows is parenthetical—that it provides additional information not necessary in identifying the noun.

> *I gave the baseball to Bob Jones, **who collects baseballs**.*
> *Mary Jones, **who was elected cheerleader**, was happy.*
> *Mary Jones, **elected cheerleader**, was happy.*
> *Mary Jones, **forgetting about her sore leg**, ran to answer the phone.*
> *Jason Gomez, **angry about how little he was making after working such long hours**, quit his job.*
> Justin, ***who is a computer programmer***, is paid well.
> *Justin, **a computer programmer**, is paid well.*

Exercise 1
Is a comma needed at the place or places underlined? Explain why or why not.

1. The people _ lining up to buy tickets to the concert _ had brought cots and picnic baskets.

2. His mother _ who saved money for him to go to college _ was upset when he dropped out.

3. Stan Musial _ an outfielder for the St. Louis Cardinals _ was from the coal mining area of Pennsylvania.

4. The player _ elected to the Hall of Fame this year _ had the vote of Jim Bryant _ a reporter for the Chicago Tribune.

5. My teacher _ irritated by the sloppy writing that we were turning in _ threw the papers in our faces and sneered.

Punctuating Appositives.

In the last two examples above we can see how an appositive is related to the clause from which it is derived.

*Justin, **who is a computer programmer**, is paid well.*
*Justin, **a computer programmer**, is paid well.*

In the first, the *who* is the same as *the computer programmer* and the *who* is the same as *Justin*. If we take out the *who is*, we no longer have a modifying clause. Instead, we have an appositive. *Who* was the same as *Justin* and *computer programmer*, so *Justin* and *computer programmer* are now the same. We call this noun following the other noun an appositive. Because the whole *who is* clause was modifying Justin, the appositive is considered a parenthetical modifier and a comma is placed around it. But sometimes, we want the break to be more emphatic and employ an dash to set it off.

I called Bob Jones, a friend of my father.
I needed a better doctor, someone with lots of experience dealing with arthritis.
I needed a better doctor — someone with lots of experience dealing with arthritis.

Notice that there is a difference in length between a hyphen and an dash. The dash is the wild card of punctuation marks. The hyphen is not a mark of punctuation.

Close Apposition

Some appositives are said to be in close apposition to the noun that precedes, and no comma is used to separate them from the preceding nominal phrases. Some examples are "my uncle Fred," "the coordinating conjunction *so*," "the river Jordan," and "the poet Frost."

Compounds in Modifiers of Nouns

Writing a compound modifier doesn't change how we punctuate the modifier.

We wrote a letter to a friend who moved to Boston and who is lonely.
Bob, who works hard and who never gets a vacation, is thinking about going to Boston for a weekend trip.
Tom Johnson, a fishing guide and a wine maker, lives near Point Arena.

Series in Restrictive Modifiers of Nouns

With restrictive modifiers, we do not need to change the way we punctuate the modifiers or series.

The people washing the dishes, drying them, and putting them away will not have to vacuum.

Mom inspected the dishes washed, rinsed, and dried by us.

Series in Parenthetical Modifiers of Nouns

But with parenthetical modifiers in a series there are real complications. We are using commas to set off each item in the series and also using commas to set off the parenthetical modifiers, so we have a problem. Notice the confusion if we follow the rules we have learned.

I bought my favorite fruits, bananas, apples, oranges, and grapes.
My favorite fruits, bananas, apples, oranges, and grapes, are cheap.

Commas are used to set off the appositives following *fruit* and to connect the items in the series. But commas can't be used for both purposes without confusion. What is the conventional punctuation practice for these examples? For the first example, we have a choice. We can use our wild card, the dash. Or we can use a colon in combination with the final period.

I bought my favorite fruits — bananas, apples, oranges, and grapes.
I bought my favorite fruits: bananas, apples, oranges, and grapes.

Notice that the dash and the colon here are like equal signs, showing that the fruits which follow are equal to *my favorite fruits*.
But with the second sentence, we cannot employ the colon because we need to have a separator on each side of the modifier, and colons aren't used in pairs. So we employ the dash.

My favorite fruits — bananas, apples, oranges, and grapes — are cheap.

Series With Parenthetical Modifiers of Nouns

I would have no trouble punctuating the following sentences.

My friend is Bill, an electrician.
My friend is George, a plumber.

And if I compounded them into one sentence, I would still have no trouble in punctuating the sentence.

My friends are Bill, an electrician, and George, a plumber.

But when I try to add two more friends, I have trouble because commas are used both for setting off the modifier and for separating elements of the series.

My friends are Bill, an electrician, George, a plumber, Hal, a carpenter, and Joe, a mason.

The typical way of solving the problem is inelegant at best. We use semicolons. I call the semicolon used this way a *super comma*. When it is used to separate two independent clauses, I call it a *junior period*. These are the only two uses I know of for the semicolon. It should not be used as a wild card. But even the wild card, the dash, is not used to separate items in a series containing a parenthetical. Here is the inelegant solution.

My friends are Bill, an electrician; George, a plumber; Hal, a carpenter; and Joe, a mason.

Exercise 2

Is a mark of punctuation needed at the place or places underlined? If so, which one. Explain.

1. The vegetable that I bought _ a squash _ has gone bad.

2. My two favorite vegetables _ tomatoes and okra _ are good together.

3. His three favorite cars _ the Edsel, the Studebaker, and the LaSalle _ are no longer being manufactured.

4. He lied to three of my friends _ Carl, Mary, and Michelle.

5. The students _ talking to _ Michael, Mary, and Michelle are trying to get them to go to tonight's game.

6. While Guy Thibodeaux is eating my two favorite Cajun foods _ dirty rice and gumbo _ I am watching him with envy.

End- and Front-Shifted Parentheticals

Some of the parenthetical noun modifiers can be moved from their usual position after the nouns to the front or end of the sentence. The clauses introduced by *who, whom,* or *which* cannot be moved. The appositive is rarely moved, but adjective phrases, present-participle phrases, and past-participle phrases rather frequently appear at the first and last of sentences. They are then routinely set off by commas.

Bob Robinson, happy about his promotion, celebrated.

Happy about his promotion, Bob Robinson celebrated.

Bob Robinson bought a house, sure that he could make the monthly payments.

Mary Jones, forgetting about her sore leg, ran to answer the phone.

Forgetting about her sore leg, Mary Jones ran to answer the phone.

She worked hard, staying at the computer from dawn to dark.

Our team, defeated by a superior opponent, returned eagerly to the practice field.

Defeated by a superior opponent, our team returned eagerly to the practice field.

She worked hard, driven by a desire to succeed.

Even when commas are in these phrases because of a series, the comma is usually sufficient to set them off.

Worrying about his clothes, fearing the committee's disapproval, and hoping for the best, Pete went into the interview.

Pete went into the interview, worrying about his clothes, fearing the committee's disapproval, and hoping for the best.

Lesson 4   35

But I have seen good writers separate such parenthetical series from the main clause with a dash.

Old, angry, and tired — Bob Wilson resigned.

He sat there — remembering what mattered in his life, knowing that he had many good years left, considering his options.

Semicolons are not used to set these series off from the main clause. And colons rarely serve that purpose. Occasionally a parenthetical phrase is not set off from the verb even by a comma.

I ate standing.

These various parentheticals can appear mixed in all three positions and are each set off from the other with a comma.

Happy about winning, feeling lucky still, Sue Simpson stayed in the game.

Tim Todd baked biscuits, careful to watch the temperature, keeping his eye on the clock, determined not to burn them again.

Another construction similar to these and also parenthetical is called a nominative absolute. It is set off by a comma, too.

He stood there, his eye on the thermometer.

He walked, his arms swinging lazily at his side.

He stood there, his shirt dirty, his hair hanging in his eyes, his mouth open, not looking at us, unaware that his fate was soon to be decided.

His face burned from the summer sun, John looked for shade.

The sun beating down, the buzzards circling high overhead, the dessert completely quiet, the wagons continued slowly to the west.

The nominative absolute, as you see here, is a noun with some kind of modifier It appears in the same context as the subject of the main clause. It may also appear in combination with the other parentheticals.

Exercise 3
Is a mark of punctuation needed at the place or places underlined? If so, which one. Explain.

1. Happy that I had won the first set _ I continued to rush the net.

2. My eyes tired from working so long _ I closed the book.

3. My favorite sports _ ping pong, basketball, and softball _ are not usually dangerous sports.

4. I like _ apples, oranges, bananas, and pears.

5. I _ suspicious of his intent _ decided to follow him.

6. My favorite cars _ the Lexus and the Infiniti _ are comfortable _ dependable _ and expensive.

7. I like _ Fred _ the carpenter _ and Bill _ the electrician.

8. My uncle _ Bob _ said that he wanted me to have a raise _ and a vacation _ and said that he thought that I would get them some year.

9. Although Bob had recommended me for the raise and vacation _ I didn't expect them _ because the big boss _ my father-in-law _ didn't like me.

10. Rex _ my orthodontist _ Bill _ my radiologist _ Randy _ my general practitioner _ and Sue _ my podiatrist _ pay high liability insurance.

11. The students _ eating, drinking, and playing in the mall _ appear happy.

12. He is studying four subjects _ English, algebra economics, and philosophy.

Lesson 5

Punctuating Other Parentheticals

In the previous lesson you learned to punctuate parentheticals derived from noun modifiers. These words, phrases, and clauses are called nonrestrictive because they do not identify the noun being modified but provide additional information, information which may be completely off the subject. The information most off the subject may even be set off in parentheses. If the information is even further off the subject, writers may choose to use a footnote or endnote to provide it in order not to interrupt the flow of their sentences.

We will deal with several different kinds of parentheticals in this lesson. They are most commonly set off from the main clause by a comma, but we will see some variety in this.

Punctuating Conjunctive Adverbs

Conjunctive adverbs provide the same kind of information about logical relationships between sentences as do the coordinating conjunctions and VMCIs we studied earlier. Unlike them, conjunctive adverbs do not have to introduce the structure but may be placed within or at the end of the it. They are conventionally set off by commas.

I lost the game. However, I didn't give up.
I lost the game. I, however, didn't give up.
I lost the game. I didn't give up, however.

A common error of beginning writers is to punctuate these sentences as if the conjunctive adverb is a coordinating conjunction. This error leads to what teachers call a comma splice.

I lost the game, however I didn't give up.

Some teachers recommend that students avoid this comma splice by placing a semicolon between the two independent clauses.

I lost the game; however, I didn't give up.

I rarely see this done in print, so I believe the best way to make it conventional is to use a period and a capital letter and start a new sentence.

Here is a list of common conjunctive adverbs.

afterwards, also, concurrently, consequently, hence, henceforth, hereafter, however, later, meantime, meanwhile, moreover, nevertheless, next, nonetheless, once, otherwise, then, thereafter, therefore, though, thus, too

The conjunctive adverb *though* can be easily confused with the VMCI *though*, a shortened form of *although*. They are obviously punctuated differently.

Though I lost the game, I didn't give up.
I lost the game. I didn't give up, though.

Notice that *though* in the first sentence cannot be replaced by the conjunctive adverb *however*, but the one in the second can. The *though* in the first sentence can be replaced by the VMCI *although*, but the one in the second can't.

Often beginning writers confuse the conjunctive adverb with a coordinating conjunction at the first of a sentence, so they mistakenly put commas after coordinating conjunctions. Neither VMCIs nor coordinating conjunctions at the first of a sentence should have commas following them.

I worked hard. And I got a raise
I worked hard. But I didn't get a raise.
I worked hard. Yet I didn't get a raise.
I worked hard. So I got a raise.

Some teachers teach their students not to begin sentences with coordinating conjunctions. But almost all of our best writers use them frequently and well at the first of sentence.

The only time when a comma comes immediately after the coordinating conjunction is when it is followed by some kind of parenthetical.

I took the daily paper. But, of course, I worked so hard that I had no time to read it.

Exercise 1.
Punctuate the following sentence. Start a new sentence if necessary to prevent a comma splice. Some sentences may need no additional punctuation.

1. I was happy in college yet I missed my dog.
2. I was happy in college nevertheless I missed my dog.

Lesson 5   39

3. I was happy in college but I missed my dog.
4. I was happy in college however I missed my dog.
5. I was happy in college I however missed my dog.
6. I was happy in college I missed my dog however.
7. Though I was happy in college I missed my dog.
8. I was happy in college though I missed my dog.
9. I was happy in college I missed my dog though.
10. I liked running moreover it was good for me.
11. I was happy in college. But I missed my dog.
12. I was happy in college. But of course I missed my dog.

Some writers will sometime not set off conjunctive adverbs in order to give them less emphasis. Some short conjunctive adverbs, notably *then* and *also*, are often not set off by commas.

Punctuating Prepositional Phrases that are like Conjunctive Adverbs

There are a group of prepositional phrases that function like conjunctive adverbs and are punctuated in the same way.

Gilbert Smithers was successful at work. On the other hand, his home life was a disaster.
Gilbert Smithers was successful at work. His home life, on the other hand, was a disaster.
Gilbert Smithers was successful at work. His home life was a disaster, on the other hand.

Here is a list of prepositional phrases functioning like conjunctive adverbs.

after this, as a result, as a result of this, as a substitute, as an alternative, at this time, because of this, despite that, despite this, for a week, for that reason, from this time, in a way that accords with that, in accordance, in accordance with that, in addition, in addition to that, in conclusion, in contrast, in contrast to that, in lieu of that, in place of that, in spite of that, in summary, in summation, in that case, in that event, in time, instead of that, no doubt, of course, on occasions, on the other hand, since that time, since then, under those circumstances, within the hour

Exercise 2

Punctuate the following sentence. Start a new sentence if necessary to prevent a comma splice. Some sentences may need no additional punctuation.

1. I like movies but I don't like violent movies.
2. I worked hard I as a result got a raise.
3. I worked hard as a result I got a raise.
4. I worked hard I got a raise as a result.
5. I was washing dishes Mary meanwhile was sweeping.
6. I was washing dishes meanwhile Mary was sweeping.
7. I was washing dishes Mary at the same time was sweeping.
8. I was washing dishes Mary was sweeping at the same time.
9. I worked hard. Yet I didn't get a raise.

Nouns in Direct Address

Nouns in direct address are set off by commas. These are unlikely to cause any writers trouble. They rarely appear in formal writing unless important speeches are being reproduced.

Bob, behave yourself.
My fellow Americans, now is the time to do something about our lack of oil production.
You will be punished, Bob, unless you behave.

Adverbials of Attitude, Context, Style

Like the conjunctive adverbs, these are set off, by commas commonly at the first of sentences.

Apparently, there will be a test today.
Of course, I will be there.
Sadly, we lost.
Frankly, I don't care.
Well, I could care less.
Generally, we avoid the discussion.
Briefly, we must conserve energy.

Exercise 3

Punctuate the following. Some may need no punctuation.

1. Unhappily I can't go to the party.

2. However I can meet some of you afterwards.

3. But I will be in my work clothes.

4. Sue can you meet me?

5. Honestly I can't go.

6. I will meet you instead.

7. Well that's the best I can do.

Exercise 4

Is a mark of punctuation needed at the place or places underlined? If so, which one. Explain.

1. Bob used to work at HEB. But _ he works at Best Buy now.

2. Bob used to work at HEB. However _ he works at Best Buy now.

3. Susie lost her car key. She has a spare _ though.

4. Though _ Susie lost her car key _ she has a spare

5. Susie lost her car key. She _however _ has a spare

Lesson 6

Punctuating Quotations

Quotation marks are marks of punctuation which are used for short direct quotations. The quoted material is most commonly the direct object of a verb such as *said* or *wrote*. Normally, we don't put commas between a verb and its object, but with a quotation we do. Periods are conventionally placed inside the final quotation mark however illogical this may seem at times.

Bob Jones said, "I can't quit now."

Indirect quotations are not placed inside quotation marks, and no comma is used before the direct object.

Bob Jones said he can't quit now.

Conventionally, single quotation marks are not used unless within a direct quotation.

Bill Smith said, "My doctor said, 'Never eat before a blood test.'"

Quoted material of over a hundred words is normally indented and sometimes single spaced to indicate that it is quoted. In this case, no quotation marks are used. If there is quoted material within the quotation, the double quotation marks rather than the single ones are used. Writers of some texts and some style manuals have other requirements in length for blocking quotes. Some say four lines. Others say as many as ten before the quotation is blocked.

When a complete sentence precedes quoted material, a colon is the conventional mark of punctuation.

He repeated his earlier assertion: "I am innocent."

Occasionally a dash will be used after the complete introduction prior to the quoted material.

Like periods, commas conventionally are placed inside the quotation marks.

"Our country must have new leadership," the candidate insisted.

"Our country," the candidate said, "must have new leadership."

With question marks, the placement depends on what is in question. Sometimes it is inside, sometimes out.

Bob asked, "Who's going to the movie tonight?"
Did you say, "Let me out of here"?
Did you say, "Who's going to the movie tonight?"

If only the quoted material is a question, the question mark goes inside the quotation marks If the whole sentence is a question but not the quotation, the question mark goes outside. If both are questions, the question mark goes inside.

Exclamation points go inside quotation marks.

He said, "What a throw!"

If a quotation is the subject of a sentence, it is not separated from the verb by a period or a comma.

"Eat more beef" is the motto of the cattlemen.

If the quotation is a subject and a question or exclamation, the question mark and the exclamation point are placed inside the quotation marks.

"Will we survive?" is what we asked ourselves.
"What a catch!" is what the announcer hollered.

Colons and semicolons that follow a quotation are conventionally placed outside the quotation marks.

Katherine Anne Porter wrote "The Grave"; William Sydney Porter wrote "The Cop and the Anthem."
Katherine Anne Porter wrote "The Grave" and "Noon Wine": two excellent short stories set in Hays County.

Sometimes quotation marks are not used to show that the material inside them is quoted. Instead, they indicate the writer giving a special emphasis to a word. These are called 'scare' quotes. Often single quotes are used for them, but almost as often "scare" quote writers use double quotes for them. College writing handbooks usually show double quotes for them. Some writers put commas and periods inside them. Others put them outside.

44 Purposeful Punctuation

He's a regular 'jabbermouth'.
They called that little shack a "spa," and they wanted us to stay there.

Exercise

Is a mark of punctuation needed at the place or places underlined? If so, which one. Explain.

1. I said _ she was not reliable.

2. I said _ "She is not reliable _" _

3. I wrote this short apology _ "My behavior at the party was abominable _" _

4. Who said _ "Life is just a bowl of cherries _" _

5. Did he say _ "Our closest neighbor is Mars _"

6. Bill said _ "Where are you going tonight _" _

7. Did Bill say _ Where are you going tonight _" _

8. "I want _" _ he said _ "a new car _" _

9. "I will win the championship _" _ Jim said.

10. "I don't like Ike _" _ is what we chanted last year.

11. Who won _ was _ what we all asked.

Lesson 6   45

Lesson 7

Punctuating Exclamations

Many young writers love the exclamation point and employ it with great regularity and enthusiasm in their writing, particularly in letters home.

Send money!!!!!!!! Now!!!!

But it should be used with restraint in careful writing. There are three kinds of sentence in which it is the only appropriate end punctuation. Here are examples of the three.

Ouch!
What a beautiful baby!
How smart you are!

In addition to these, important and forceful commands are usually ended by an exclamation mark.

Get out!
Never remove the pot from the oven without a hot pad!

Otherwise, I don't use them in careful writing, and I advise my students not to, insisting that there are better ways to let the reader know what I think is important, what is worth emphasis.

Exclamation marks go inside quoted material.

He said, "How smart you are!"

Exercise
Employ exclamation points conservatively and conventionally in closing the following sentences.
1. What a nice day
2. I really like flowers
3. How nice your new hair style is
4 What was the answer to number one
5. Quit smoking
6. Wow
7. He said Ouch

46   Purposeful Punctuation

Lesson 8

The Wild Card — The Dash

In the previous lessons, I have presented information about the conventional ways of punctuating English sentences, but that is hardly the whole story about punctuation. Skillful professional writers who know these conventions well often choose to vary from them in order to accomplish a different writing purpose. They are particularly fond of using dashes to do that.

I wrote an essay several years ago for a seminar on John Graves at the Southwestern Writers Collection at Texas State University. The essay deals with the similarity between John Graves and E. B. White, particularly in their sense of independence and their use of dashes. The essay was later published in a special issue of *Southwestern American Literature* about John Graves and in the book, *John Graves, Writer*, edited by Mark Busby and Terrell Dixon (University of Texas Press, 2007). I am providing it here to illustrate how varied the use of the dash can be.

Of Dachshunds and Dashes:
Subjects and Style in E. B. White and John Graves

I looked forward to writing this essay once I decided on my subject because I have read with pleasure and taught with even more pleasure the works of E. B. White and John Graves. For over forty years, I have been teaching White's essay "Once More to the Lake." With freshman class after freshman class, I have been back and back and back, to Belgrade Lake in Maine. Almost as often, I have taught Graves' *Goodbye to a River*, mostly to Southwestern literature and nature writing classes. I have selected these and other works by these writers because I like what they write about and how they write about it. Graves and White have many things in common. They began their successful writing careers by publishing in the *New Yorker* — White with a regular column and Graves with a short story. They left the city to live in rural areas and write about their lives there. White moved from New York City to North Brooklin, Maine in 1938 and wrote a regular column for *Harper's*. From it, he selected essays to produce his *One Man's Meat* and later the collection *Second Tree from the Corner*. Graves moved from Fort Worth to his land near Glen Rose, Texas. He wrote *Hard Scrabble* about his life there, and he wrote essays for *Texas Monthly*, selecting from these to fill his collection *From a Limestone Ledge*.

White lived on the extremely cold Maine coast, north of Bar Harbor, Graves in extremely hot Texas, yet they found common subjects to write about, particularly the animals they owned. Of the many animals they wrote about, the ones that most interest me are the dachshunds because I own and have owned dachshunds, right now two standard, wirehaired littermates, Barnaby and Clementine. The breed was developed in Germany and bred with short legs and powerful neck and shoulders to enable the dogs to go into holes and fight badgers. Because there are no humans down in the holes to help the dogs in this pursuit, the most successful dogs, and thus the breed, had to develop a high degree of independence and determination. Though not called on to hunt badgers here in the States, the breed has maintained those characteristics. About my dachshunds, I can tell many stories—but won't. But I will quote my wife, Andrea, who says—sagely: "You don't see dachshunds in obedience competition." E. B. White said much the same thing when he wrote:

> Being the owner of dachshunds, to me a book on dog discipline becomes a volume of inspired humor. Every sentence is a riot. Someday, if I ever get a chance, I shall write a book, or warning, on the character and temperament of the Dachshund and why he can't be trained and shouldn't be. I would rather train a zebra to balance an Indian club than induce a dachshund to heed my slightest command. When I address Fred I never have to raise either my voice or my hopes. He even disobeys me when I instruct him in something he wants to do. (*One Man's Meat*, 160)

In another essay also in *One Man's Meat*, White tells us more about the behavior of Fred:

> Here he awaits the fall of an egg to the floor and the sensual delight of licking it up — which he does with lips drawn slightly back as though in distaste at the strange consistency of the white. His hopes run always to accidents and misfortunes: the broken egg, the spilt milk, the wounded goose, the fallen lamb, the fallen cake. His activities and his character constitute an almost uninterrupted annoyance to me, yet he is such an engaging old fool that I am quite attached to him, in a half-regretful way. Life without him would be heaven, but I'm afraid it is not what I want. (264)

John Graves, in talking about Blue and other dogs he had owned, mentions his concept of the "Nice Dog." Then he says that his dog Watty, a dachshund, was "emphatically not one" (*John Graves Reader*, 225). He goes on to tell about his Watty, also known as Passenger, Cacahuate, and Peanut:

> He started out all right, intelligent and affectionate and as willing to learn as dachshunds ever are, and with the nose he had he made a fair retriever, albeit hardmouthed with shot birds and inclined to mangle them a bit before reluctantly giving them up. He was fine company too, afield or in a canoe or a car, and we had some good times together. But his temper started souring when I married and grew vile when children came, and the job was finished by a paralyzing back injury with a long painful recovery, never complete, and by much sympathetic spoiling along the way. As an old lame creature, a stage that lasted at least five years, he snarled, bit, disobeyed, stank more or less constantly and from time to time broke wind to compound it, yowled and barked for his supper in the kitchen for two hours before feeding time, subverted the good sheep dogs' training, and was in general the horrid though small-scale antithesis of a Nice Dog. And yet in replication of my childhood self I loved him, and buried him wrapped in a feed sack beneath a flat piece of limestone with his name scratched deep upon it. (225)

Much of what Scott Elledge, White's biographer, said about White's attachment to his dachshund might also apply to that of Graves:

> During the many years that Fred had been his close companion, White had attributed to him a rich and real personality. Fred was "vile," gluttonous, and lascivious, possessing a "heavy charge of original sin." He was incapable of human love or loyalty, and he tended to deflate rather than build up his master's ego. But White admired him because he was "intensely loyal to himself, as every strong individualist must be," and because he loved life and was driven by curiosity. In Fred's individualism, in his loyalty to himself, and in his love of life and curiosity about it, White saw much of White. . . . (277)

White was an independent person even as a young man, one wanting to live and write for himself, to choose his own path, unfettered by rules. About criticism of his manuscript of *Stuart Little* by Anne Carroll Moore, children's librarian emerita of the New York Public Library, White wrote:

Her letter was long, friendly, urgent, and thoroughly surprising. She said she had read proofs of my forthcoming book called *Stuart Little* and advised me to withdraw it. She said, as I recall the letter, that the book was non-affirmative, inconclusive, unfit for children, and would harm its author if published. These were strong words and I was grateful to Miss Moore for having taken the trouble to write them. I thought the matter over, however, and decided that as long as the book satisfied me, I wasn't going to let an expert talk me out of it. It is unnerving to be told you're bad for children, but I detected in Miss Moore's letter an assumption that there are rules governing the writing of juvenile literature — rules as inflexible as the rules for lawn tennis. And this I was not sure of. I had followed my instincts in writing about Stuart, and following one's instincts seemed to be the way a writer should operate. (Quoted in Elledge, 263)

Given his fondness for independence, I find it surprising that White would have found the "rules" for writing in William Strunk's 1918 little book something to admire, but he did. When he revised *Elements of Style,* he made many changes. Strunk's precepts were not his. Elledge quotes White as saying that he could not "don the robes of solemnity at this late date" (330) and as saying that he did his own writing "by ear and seldom with any idea of what was taking place under the hood" (326). In his revision of *Elements of Style*, White wrote:

> The beginner should approach style warily, realizing that it is himself he is approaching, no other; and he should begin by turning resolutely away from all devices that are popularly believed to indicate style — all mannerisms, tricks, adornments. The approach to style is by way of plainness, simplicity, orderliness, sincerity. (Strunk, 69)

William Strunk's third "elementary rule of usage" was "Enclose parenthetic expressions between commas." And that is the generic way of doing it. But among the other possible ways are, of course, enclosing them between parentheses, when they are quite off the subject, or between colons and periods. But the way preferred by writers who most frequently use parenthetical structures is to use paired dashes or a dash with a closing mark of punctuation. The dash allows the writer to announce boldly that he is going away from the main subject, that he is chasing rabbits. Dachshunds would love dashes. Using dashes is a declaration of independence, a way for the writer to put into his composition all of the nitty-gritty little things that make life interesting, whether near Glen Rose or Blue Hill. A dachshund, in a hole alone, must decide for itself how to fight a badger — must be independent, resourceful. Just so, must a writer be. Graves and White, exceptionally able, experienced, and competent writers, did not listen to arbiters of correctness, such as Ann Carroll Moore or William Strunk, did not follow their rules. Instead, Graves, a Texan, and White, a Mainer, each thought for himself, each a Maverick, seeking to and succeeding in writing clear, highly textured prose. Each found the dash an exceptional tool, allowing them to provide the many asides that enliven their prose.

Examples Showing Use of the Dash
by John Graves in *Goodbye to a River*

Apposition

His Hernan Cortez was a man named Peter Garland — Captain Garland, they called him. (48)

Like someone in Tolstoy — Levin's brother, was it? — I'm fond of angling . . . . (208)

Feelings without knowledge — love, and hatred, too — seem to flow easily in any time. . . . (4)

But the squabbling had begun between their proponents and those otherwise-minded types — bottomland farmers and ranchers whose holdings would be inundated, competitive utility companies shrilling "Socialism!" and big irrigationists downstream — who would make a noise before they lost, but who would lose. (9)

 He piled papers and maps on me, and instructions to see things he knew of and to look for things whose existence he suspected — Indian sites, beavers, and eaten-away silt cliff where longhorns' skulls and the remains of bison still came occasionally to view. (11)

I . . . finally carried up the other things from the boat — the map case and the shotgun and the rods and the food box, heavily full, and the cook box and the rucksack, all of them battered familiarly from other trips long before. (15)

There was very little Hollywood about them, and not much Fenimore Cooper. Rough, certainly. . . mainly Southern, but not altogether, and even the Southerners heterogeneous in origin and type — rednecks and slaveholding younger sons from the cotton states, Texas Revolutionary veterans from the older cattle counties far down the Brazos and the Colorado, hillmen from Tennessee and Carolina. (25; Graves' ellipsis)

All the murdered, scalped, raped, tortured people, red and white, all the proud names that belonged with hills and valleys and bends and crossings or maybe just hovered over the whole — Bigfoot Wallace, Oliver Loving, Charles Goodnight, Cynthia Ann Parker and her Indian son Quanah, Peta Nocona, Satank, Satanta, Iron Shirt. . . (7; Graves' ellipsis)

Nominative Absolute (Before a Relative Clause)

It was of that ungothic shape — roof peaked high along a ridge pole in the middle over three rooms in a row, and flattening fore and aft over the gallery and a rank of lean-to room — which the double log cabins form had suggested to a log-cabin people abruptly presented with lumber. (69)

Extended Series of Prepositional Phrases

They lack the absoluteness of the spacious, disappearing breeds — of geese riding the autumn's southward thrust, of eagles, of grizzlies, of bison I never saw except in compounds. . . Of wolves. . . Of wild horses that have been hunted down in twenty years or so and have been converted into little heaps of dog dung on the nations mowed lawns. And antelope, and elk grazing among the high aspens, an old bull always on guard. . . (29; Graves' ellipses)

What other brand of godliness, though, would you have substituted for it — in that time, in that place, in that people? (191)

Qualifying/Contrasting

We river-minded ones can't say much against them — nor, probably, should we want to. Nor, mostly, do we. . . . (8; Graves' ellipsis)

In that case they'd be letting out more — probably too much, he said ironically. (13)

It was a kind of tangential retribution for Moctezuma and the burned libraries of the Mayas — not that the Comanches thought of working retribution far anyone's wrongs but their own. . . . (19)

I would have been a headless-burgoo man — in fact am. . . . (33)

But it could be true — ought to be. . . . (62; Graves' ellipsis)

"Please, Buenas Noches," maybe one of them said. Maybe not — The People seldom begged. (63)

Change. Autumn. Maybe — certainly — there was melancholy in it, but it was a good melancholy. (119)

Another time on the Guadalupe to the south — but this is supposed to be about the Brazos . . . . (161; Graves' ellipsis)

"Aw, naw," Bill Briggs would say mildly when we wanted to do something we had no business doing, like — tired of fishing — swimming in the river when it was running strong, or — tired of fish — swiping a pullet from a farmer's flock, or — tired of chopping hard resistant driftwood — trying out our ax on the big shade trees above the bank. (250-251)

Parenthetical

From there Hale and I — he was taking me out — drove across the stripped and eroded farming section. . . . (12)

They . . . left place names and casks and chests of gold at each night's stopping place — "Ef a man only had him a good witchin' stick" — but for the most part who they were and how many and when is unknowable. . . . (17)

Irked perhaps by my calm — people who fly around near the ground seem to require delight and awe from earthbound watchers — they banked into a tight circle and came back to buzz me. . . . (27-28)

There was a fine long piece of river below, deep but with a pull, and running somehow — a miracle-sidewise to the wind, so that the water next to one bank was sheltered and smooth. (31)

The big water scooted us on down — I know the "us" is an anthropomorphism, but in the absence of other company a dog makes a plural, and not a bad one either — and through a fine, pounding rapids. . . . (42)

Noun Modifying (Adjectival)

He was a six-month-old dachshund and weighed about twelve pounds, and even after he was grown he wouldn't be a very practical dog, but he was company, too — more concrete, perhaps, than memories and feelings. (16)

So that the pathos one is prone to see in their destruction — apart, different from the destructions of the other red peoples to the east — is not pathos at all . . . . (20)

But the river was pretty where I was — wide and clean and even-flowing, with curious, arching, limestone overhanging along the right shore — and after the rain had stopped I dawdled. . . . (43-44)

Interrupter between Preposition and Its Object (Single Dash)

If one had a modern-tragic view like — oh, Graham Greene's, one might make symbols our of those fingers. (121)

Repetition of Verbs

Then, within a century, they made themselves into one of history's great races of riders — and made riders too of the other plains tribes northward and westward to whom they traded ponies. (18)

Implied Causation

Skating about the canoe on clogged boot soles, I made the laborious rearrangements and tied things down again and tarped them again and then, unwilling to start out again in the day's unpromising monotony — it seemed somehow a waste of good river — walked followed by the pup into the valley above the crossing. (25)

And the claim did have a little poetic verity — the river winds hugely. (77)

Ewell knew, but one finds it hard to blame him — writing in Granbury, with that kind of people still around him — for not having set it down. (203)

People with children — it was Sunday — walked along a path by the river and looked at me. (291)

Setting Off Adverbial Clause

And I care about knowing what it is, and — if I can — why. (160)

Setting Off Direct Object

They tell too — the stories — of the subsequent squabbles among the louts themselves. (143)

Repetition of Subject and Verb

It knifes through you, for instance, after waiting through a long golden evening for doves beside a stock tank in someone's pasture, watching your first bird coming in high and swift on the north wind, laying down knowing before you fire that you are on him, watching him contract raggedly and fall in a long parabola to baked hard earth and then going to pick him up — it knifes to feel suddenly in his warmth against your palm, in the silk touch of the feathers at his throat, all the pity of that perished gentle wildness. . . . (54; Graves' ellipsis)

Examples Showing Use of the Dash
by E. B. White in *One Man's Meat*

Relative Clause

These persons are feared by every tyrant — who shows his fear by burning the books and destroying the individuals. (139)

Relative Clause Complementing a Verb Phrase

I got out of bed at half-past six, thinking about dreams and about what a plowman had told me the other day — which was that he often gets the answer to his problems in dreams. He had a dream lately telling him what to do about my newly-laid-down field, where I didn't get a very good catch of grass. (192)

Relative Clause Complementing a Location

One morning a few months ago, during a particularly busy time, when I awoke I didn't dare get dressed: I knew that my only hope of getting an overdue piece written was to stay in bed — which is where I did stay. (141)

Apposition

 From these animals and this land you will receive all the food you and your family need, plus forty dollars a month — $25 from eggs, $15 from cream. (142)

This protein is ordinarily provided (on profit-and loss farms) by expensive concentrates bought at a grain store — laying mash, hog ration, etc. (143)

So down the back stairs noisily and out through the dewy field with Fred, my chore dog, to the chicken range, where I opened the doors of the shelters and watched my two hundred pullets, long pent up, come sailing through the openings like chaff on the wind — a black cloud of feathers and delight. (193)

You will be looking out of a window, say, at a tree; and then after a bit the tree won't be there any more, and the looking won't be there any more, only the window will be there, in memory — the thing through which the looking has been done. (193)

The fourth, fifth, and sixth graders were gathered in the schoolyard with their teacher, who had on trousers in honor of the event, and I wished that I could see again (and in trousers) some of the teachers I had had in grammar school — Miss Hackett and Miss Kirby and Miss Crosby and Miss Douglas and Miss Ihlefeldt and Mrs. Schuyler and Miss Abigail A. Bourne and Miss Sheridan. (194)

I being glad, as always, to be self-released from indoor work and glad to be visiting the old Herrick place, which is remote and quiet — an old tumbledown barn in a run-out field encircled by woods and overlooking a small secluded cove. (194)

As we lifted the tongue of the roll and stirred the thing, a mouse leaped up and ran the length of it, like a tiny dog performing a circus act. I thought how pleasant it would be to start life fresh on the old Herrick place, with a one-room shack and no appurtenances — no equipment, no stock, no pets, no family responsibilities, no program. (194)

But knowing myself as well as I do, I well knew that it wouldn't be twenty minutes before I would acquire or contrive something to establish the roots of complexity in firm soil — a cold chisel perhaps, or an inamorata, or a folding towel rack. (194)

Just hulks of men, these old fellows seemed to me — dry stalks, autumnal creatures, about to die. (195)

Qualifying/Contrasting

I have a wholly different picture of doomsday — or rather doomsmoment. (193)

Noun Modifying (Adjectival)

In no time at all I would destroy the old Herrick place by setting out a pansy plant or repairing a rotten sill. And then it would be just like any other spot — beloved but not removed. (194-195)

Nominative Absolute

It was, as I had suspected, made in one long cylinder — narrow ten-foot spruce planks bolted to a pair of old mowing-machine wheels, and the frame heavily constructed. (195)

Complement to Predicate Adjective

This year we're going to try putting up rhubarb, which I am told is simple — just cold water, no processing. (196)

Series of Past Participles to Complement Main Verb

On my last trip, however, it seemed to me that people had remodeled their ideas too — taken in their convictions a little at the waist, shortened the sleeves of their resolve, and fitted themselves out in a new intellectual ensemble copied from a smart design out of the very latest page of history. (135)

Independent Clause of Summary

He added: "Our American youngsters spend all their time at the movies — they're a mess." (135)

Luckily I am not out to change the world — that's being done for me, and at a great clip. (139)

Prepositional Phrase of Time

A writer goes about his task today with the extra satisfaction that comes from knowing that he will be the first to have his head lopped of — even before the political dandies. (139)

Adverbial Clause of Contrast

Nobody knows this better than I do — although my neighbors know it well enough and on the whole have been tolerant and sympathetic. (143)

Noun Phrase

And remember also that the grain harvest comes at the same season as the canning — those 600 Mason jars that have to be filled. (144)

Appendix 1

Answers and Explanations

Lesson 1
Exercise 1

1. Bob finished his work in the lab early.

    There is no internal punctuation because the adverb *early* is in its customary place at the end of the sentence.

2. Bob may get home early if he can get to the bus on time.

    There is no internal punctuation because the verb-modifying clause *if he can get to the bus on time* is in its customary place at the end of the sentence and the VMCI *if* shows where the clause begins.

3. If I see him, I will give him your message.
    A comma comes after the verb-modifying clause introduced by *if* because it is conventional even though leaving the comma out would not cause a lack of clarity.

4. Tim stayed at the lab late so that he could finish his work.

    There is no internal punctuation because the verb-modifying clause *so that he could finish his work* is in its customary place at the end of the sentence and the VMCI *so that* shows where the clause begins.

5. So that he could finish his work, Tim stayed at the lab late.

    A comma comes after the verb-modifying clause introduced by *so that* because it is conventional even though leaving the comma out would not cause a lack of clarity.

6. As soon as Tim gets here, I will give him your message.

    As soon as is a VMCI, a subordinating conjunction which introduces an introductory clause which modifies the verb, so a comma comes after the clause.

7. When he got home, I told him what you said.

    When is one of the more common VMCIs, and it introduces a clause which has been placed out of the customary order, so a comma is needed to show where the clause ends.

8. In addition to the fact that he failed to put out the dog, he didn't turn off the lights.

A comma comes after *dog*, There are many VMCIs which end with *the fact that*. Most of them should be replaced by the more common and less wordy VMCIs. For example, *owing to the fact that* can be replaced by *because*, and *in spite of the fact that* can be replaced by *although*. But there is no other VMCI of addition to substitute for *in addition to the fact that*.

9. He will eat more ice cream although he said that he wouldn't.

   There is no internal punctuation because the verb-modifying clause *although he said that he wouldn't* is in its customary place at the end of the sentence and the VMCI *although* shows where the clause begins.

10. Now that I am ready to go, my ride still isn't here.

    Many compound VMCIs ending in *that* introduce clauses which modify a verb. So a comma is needed after the introductory clause.

11. So I would be eligible to play baseball, I studied every afternoon.

    So in this sentence is a shortened form of the VMCI *so that*, so a comma is needed after the introductory clause.

Exercise 2

1. Hal, when he gets here, will tell you what happened.

   When is a VMCI, and the verb-modifying clause it introduces comes between the subject *Hal* and the verb *will tell*, so commas are placed around the clause.

2. Hal will tell you what happened if you ask him.

   What happened is a nominal clause direct object of *tell*. The clause introduced by *if* comes last, so no commas are needed.

3. If you ask him, Hal will tell you what happened.

   The *if* clause is at the front, so a comma is needed.

4. As I was going into the building, Hal was coming out.

   As is another common VMCI, so a comma comes after the front-shifted verb-modifying clause.

5. Although I like Margie, I don't believe that she can be trusted.

   Although is sometimes shortened to *though*, but it will not change the way the sentence is punctuated. A comma comes after the front-shifted verb-modifying clause.

6. Trees, when they are planted in the summer, will need lots of water if it doesn't rain.

The *when* clause comes between the subject *trees* and the verb *will need*, so it is set off by commas. No comma is needed before the final *if* clause.

Exercise 3

1. To get to Austin from here, I sometimes take Post Road.

    Infinitive phrases of reason, which modify the verb, are followed by commas when they appear first.

2. I should wash my hair more often so that it will look better when I go out on a date.

    The two verb-modifying clauses introduced by *so that* and *when* are in their customary places following the verbs, so no commas are needed.

3. In order to make enough money to pay tuition, he has to work at two jobs.

    In order is a common introducer of an infinitive phrase of reason. Sometimes *so as to* is used to introduce the phrase, but I think it is too informal for high informal prose. With either one, a comma comes after the infinitive phrase of reason when it is placed at the front.

4. The school, in order to attract more basketball fans, is giving discounts on the tickets.

    The infinitive phrase of reason comes between the subject, *the school,* and the verb, *is giving, so commas are needed.*

5. He went to the store to buy milk.

    No punctuation is needed because the infinitive phrase is after the verb it modifies.

Exercise 4

1. He said that when he quits working at the grocery store, he will take a vacation.

    That and all that follows is the direct object of *said*. Inside the *that* clause, the verb-modifying *when* clause comes before the main clause, so it must be followed by a comma.

2. I hope you remember where you put the tools.

    Every thing after *hope* is the direct object. *That* is the understood subordinating conjunction which could introduce it. The adverbial *where* clause comes last, so no comma is needed before it.

3. In order to speak proper French, I had to learn that if the verb was in the future tense, I should join the whole infinitive with the future endings.

> A comma is needed after the infinitive of reason introduced by *in order to*. Everything after *that* is the direct object of *learn*. In the *that* clause, the adverbial *if* clause appears before the main clause, so a comma is needed after it.

4. I know that when Bob is playing, every game leads to an argument.

> The *that* clause is the direct object of *know*. Inside it the adverbial *when* clause appears before the main clause, so a comma is needed after it.

5. He suspects that I will win the match if he serves poorly.

> The *that* clause is the direct object of *suspects*. No comma is needed because the adverbial *if* clause follows the verb of the main clause.

6. He thinks that if I whisper, I am lying.

> The *that* clause is the direct object of *thinks*. In it the verb-modifying clause introduced by *if* appears before the main clause, so a comma is needed after it.

7. I know that Bob Jones, when he is serving well, can beat me.

> The *that* clause is the direct object of *know*. The verb-modifying clause introduced by *when* appears between the subject *Bob Jones* and the verb *can beat*, so commas are needed around it.

8. I think that he will be back later although he said that he wouldn't.

> There is no internal punctuation because the verb-modifying clause *although he said that he wouldn't* is in its customary place at the end of the sentence and the VMCI *although* shows where the clause begins.

Lesson 2
Exercise 1
1. Bob has been visiting his sister in Terre Haute and plans to return by the beginning of September.

> In this sentence, there is a compound verb phrase. Bob is the subject of two verbs, *has been visiting* and *plans*. Notice there is no subject before plans, so this is not a compound clause, so no punctuation is needed.

2. Jim wants to date Mary, and Jill wants to date Jim.

> Without the comma following *Mary*, readers would think at first that Jim wanted to date both Mary and Jill. The comma tells the reader that there is not a compound direct object. Instead, there are compound independent clauses requiring a comma before the coordinating conjunction, *and*.

3. I went to the movie to see a horror picture, and I wasn't scared at all.

> Here we have compound independent clauses requiring a comma.

4. The relief pitcher entered the game in the ninth inning and picked up a save.

> Notice that there is not a subject in front of *picked*, so this is not two independent clauses. Instead, there are two verbs, so no comma is needed.

5. Sue took a class that required her to get up at six and one that kept her at school until eleven.

> Here we have two direct objects of *took*: *a class* with its modifiers and *one* with its modifier, so no comma is needed.

6. I hope that Bill will remember his old friends when he invites people to his party, and I hope he invites some new friends.

> Here the writer has chosen to repeat *I hope*, so she has written compound clauses rather than compound direct objects introduced by *that*. Had she not repeated *I hope*, there would have been no comma. Because she did, a comma is needed to separate the two independent clauses.

7. Bob stopped playing the guitar and began playing the banjo.

> Neither *Bob* nor *He* is placed before *began*, so it is a simple compound verb, and no punctuation is needed.

8. Bob can now play a banjo and a guitar well, and he will start work on a cello soon.

> There is no comma after *banjo* because there is just a compound noun phrase. And the *he* before *will start* makes these compound independent clauses rather than compound verbs, so a comma is needed.

Exercise 2

1. When Bob came home and said that he would take out the garbage and he liked doing it, everyone was surprised.

> Inside the *when* clause there are two dependent *that* clauses which tell what he said and are direct objects of *said*. The *that* between *and* and *he liked* has been omitted. Still no comma is needed there. But a comma is required to set off the *when* clause from *everyone was surprised* because of the front-shifted verb-modifying clause.

2. When Bob arrived early and when he started right to work, everyone was surprised.

No comma is needed between the two dependent adverbial *when* clauses, but because they have been front shifted, one is needed after *work*.

3. I am sure that he wanted us to stay at home if it rained and that we were right to do it.

   No comma is needed because *if it rained* comes as an adverbial at the end of the first *that* clause complementing *sure*. No comma is needed after *rained* because there are just two dependent *that* clauses.

4. I talked to him even though I didn't like him and even though he was rude to me.

   No commas are needed because there are just two verb-modifying clauses and because they are in their customary place at the end.

5. Bob knows how to repair a car with a bad muffler and how to do it with used parts.

   No commas are needed because there are just two adverbial infinitive phrases and they are in their customary place at the end.

6. She likes to write a blog and read comments about her ideas.

   No comma is needed because these are compound infinitives even though the second *to* before *read* has been omitted.

7. Some people have too much time and too much money, and they often try to find ways to keep from being bored.

   No comma is needed between the compound direct objects *too much time* and *too much money*, but one is needed between the two independent clauses connected by *and*.

8. I suspect she likes him and they will get married.

   No commas are needed because *she likes him* and *they will get married* are direct object *that* clauses serving as direct objects of *suspect*. The *that*s are understood.

9. She likes him, and they will get married.

   A comma is needed between the two independent clauses connected by *and*

10. I figured they would stop trying to get along and decide to separate.

    No comma is needed because there are just two verb phrases in the dependent clause. *Would* is understood in the second.

Exercise 3

1. Now that he has been working late, he is so tired he can hardly crawl into bed.

> A comma is needed after the front-shifted verb-modifying clause. But no comma is needed before the *so*, which is part of the *so ... that* construction which modifies *tired*. The *that* part of the construction has been omitted, and no comma is needed to show the omission.

2. He has been working late, so he is not only tired but sleepy.

> A comma is needed to separate the two independent clauses connected by the coordinating conjunction *so*. Notice that it can be paraphrased by *therefore* and that you can't place a *that* after it as you could with the VMCI. No comma is needed before *but* because it is not separating independent clauses.

3. Because of his affection for Marie and because of his dislike of her mother, Bob comes to see Marie but avoids her mother if it is possible.

> No comma is needed between the two prepositional phrases introduced by *because of*. But a comma would follow the first *mother* because of the two long introductory prepositional phrases. There is no comma before *but* because what follows is a verb phrase, not an independent clause.

4. Tim completed his degree in three years, but he wishes he had not hurried, for he fears he learned less than he might have.

> There is a comma before *but* because an independent clause both precedes and follows it. And there is a comma before *for* because an independent clause precedes and follows it. No comma is needed to indicate the omission of *that* following *fears*. No comma should follow the second *mother* because the VMCI *if* introduces a verb-modifying clause in its normal place.

5. Joe worked long hours for poor wages for years, for he needed the money for his mother's hospital bills.

> *For* is both a preposition and a coordinating conjunction. Only the third *for* is a coordinating conjunction followed by an independent clause. The others are prepositions, so no commas are needed.

6. I haven't seen him yet, but I heard Bill moved back into town, and I heard he was looking for me.

> *But* and *and* are preceded and followed by independent clauses, so commas are needed.

7. Either Bob or Tom will attend graduation or regret it.

   No commas are needed because *Bob or Tom* is a simple compound subject And *will attend* and *regret* are compound verbs. *Will* is understood before regret.

8. Many of my friends are friends of Bill and will want to see him when they have the opportunity.

   Are and *will want* are compound verbs, so no comma is needed. The *when* clause is in its customary place, so no comma precedes it.

Exercise 4

1. Bill works on Saturday from noon to midnight, but he still doesn't make much money.

   But is preceded and followed by independent clauses, so a comma is needed.

2. Though Bill works, he never seems to get ahead.

   Though is a shortened form of *although*. It is a VMCI which introduces a front-shifted verb-modifying clause, so a comma is needed after the clause.

3. Enthusiastic, healthy employees are very important to a company. They should be paid a decent wage.

   The original was a run-on sentence. A comma and the coordinating conjunction *so* could have been used to correct it also.

4. Bob's friend wants him to stop writing bad checks. He says that Bob is sure to be caught soon.

   The original was a run-on sentence. A comma and the coordinating conjunction *and* could have been used to correct it also.

5. Bill quit buying trashy novels. He didn't quit reading them. Now he goes to the library.

   The original run-on sentence had three independent clauses. After *novels*, a comma and the coordinating conjunctions *but* or *yet* could have been used.

6. Bill and Mary have problems. I think they need to go to a counselor.

   A comma and the coordinating conjunction *so* could have been used to correct it also

7. I quit my job, so now I can't pay my bills.

The coordinating conjunction *so* is preceded and followed by independent clauses. *So* could be paraphrased with *therefore*, so it is a coordinating conjunction, not the shortened form of *so that*.

8. I quit my job so I would have more time to study.

    The *so* in this sentence is not the coordinating conjunction but the VMCI. Notice that the *that* part of the connective has been omitted. So no comma is needed because the verb-modifying clause is in its customary place at the end.

9. Bob was arrested, for he passed a bad check.

    For is a coordinating conjunction preceded and followed by an independent clause. So a comma is needed.

10. Bob was arrested for passing a bad check.

    For is a preposition followed by its object *passing a bad check*. So no comma is needed.

Lesson 3
Exercise 1

1. I went to the store for milk, eggs, and bread.

    The preposition *for* has a series of three objects separated by commas.

2. I worked at Luby's, at Red Lobster, and at Sirloin Stockade.

    Commas are needed to separate the series of *at* prepositional phrases.

3. She graduated in three years and started to graduate school early.

    There are just two verbs, so there is no series, so no comma is needed.

4. She said that she liked baseball, football, and basketball, but she said that she didn't like going to the games, like watching them on TV, or like hearing her boyfriend talk about them all the time.

    Baseball, football, and basketball are a series of direct objects of *like*, so commas are needed. *But* is preceded and followed by independent clauses, so a comma precedes it. There are three verb phrases telling what she didn't like, so commas are needed to separate them.

5. The silly, infantile, and nauseating teenager made a scene in the cafeteria.

    Commas are needed to separate the series of adjectives modifying *teenager*.

6. He said I bought a bike, a car, and a golf cart, yet I didn't buy any of those. I bought a fishing rod, a reel, a fishing license.

> *A bike, a car, and a golf cart* is a series. So is *a fishing rod, a reel, a fishing license,* so commas are needed to separate them. *Yet* is preceded and followed by independent clauses, so a comma is needed.

Exercise 2

1. I talked about going to summer school or staying home.

> There are only two objects of *about,* so no comma is needed.

2. Bob likes reading, watching TV, and listening to music.

> The objects of *likes* is a series, so commas are needed

3. I hate for my roommate to lie around goofing off, to leave the dishes in the sink, and to play his music too loud.

> The three infinitive phrases are direct objects of *hate,* so commas are needed.

4. He said he knew when, where, and how to buy the best horses at the best prices.

> The three connectives words *when, where,* and *how* are introducing the single infinitive phrase, so commas are needed.

5. I hope that my son stays in school, my daughter makes good grades, and my dog does not go off hunting porcupines.

> The three *that* clauses are the direct objects of *hope,* so commas are needed. The *that*s that introduce the second and third clause have been deleted.

6. I know when my dachshunds stay home, they don't get their faces full of porcupine quills, don't get covered with skunk musk, and don't get sore paws from digging.

> Between *know* and *when* the connective word *that* is understood. It would introduce the remainder of the sentence which is the direct object of *know.* In the second clause, there are three verb phrases set off by commas. The *when* clause is shifted to the front of the verb it modifies, so a comma follows it.

7. He told me what he had done, what he would do, what he wouldn't do.

Here there are three *what* clauses functioning as direct objects of *told*. So commas are needed for the series.

8. Bob walked and talked and acted like a child.

    When *and*s appear between each element of the series, no commas are needed.

9. I can play basketball today if I don't have to keep my grandkids, if I can finish my grading, and if my wife doesn't find a job for me.

    The three *if* clauses are adverbials in their customary place after the verb, so no comma is needed to precede the first *if*, but commas are needed to mark the series.

10. He drives home from Austin, goes by the grocery store, and stops at the coffee shop.

    Commas are needed to mark the series of verb phrases.

Exercise 3

1. Bob has finished washing his car. He turned off the water, put the chamois and sponges away, and put the car back in the garage

    The original sentence was a run-on. Two independent clauses were connected with no punctuation or connective. If only a comma is placed between the independent clauses, a comma splice is created. The final independent clause has a series of three verb phrases, so commas are needed.

2. Bob has finished washing his car. He turned off the water; he put the chamois and sponges away, and he put the car back in the garage.

    The first independent clause is a summary of the three independent clauses that follow. The three clause with *he* as the subject would probably be better if the *he*s were dropped and the verb phrases were connected with commas. Less conservative writers sometimes separate the first two *he* clauses with just a comma.

3. The team played best after they practiced hard, after they ate a good meal, and after they got a good night sleep.

    The clauses following *the team played best* are all adverbial, so no comma is needed before the *after*, but a comma is needed for the series of clauses.

4. He couldn't remember where they went, what they bought, or when they left.

    The three nominal clauses function as direct objects of *remember* and are dependent, so a comma is needed to separate them.

Lesson 4
Exercise 1

1. The people lining up to buy tickets to the concert had brought cots and picnic baskets.

> The present-participle phrase *lining up to buy tickets to the concert* identifies which people had brought cots and baskets, so commas are not needed.

2. His mother, who saved money for him to go to college, was upset when he dropped out.

> The *who* clause provides additional information about someone who has already been identified, so commas are needed to set it off.

3. Stan Musial, an outfielder for the St. Louis Cardinals, was from the coal mining area of Pennsylvania.

> The proper name is sufficient to identify Musial, and the appositive, *the outfielder,* provides additional information, so it is set off with commas.

4. The player elected to the Hall of Fame this year had the vote of Jim Bryant, a reporter for the Chicago Tribune.

> The past participle phrase beginning with *elected* is necessary to identify which player, so no commas are needed to set it off. A comma is needed after Bryant because the appositive provides additional information rather than identifying him.

5. My teacher, irritated by the sloppy writing that we were turning in, threw the papers in our face and sneered.

> The past participle phrase beginning with *irritated* is not necessary to identify which teacher because *my* does the job, so no commas are needed to set it off.

Exercise 2

1. The vegetable that I bought, a squash, has gone bad.

> The single appositive should be set off by commas.

2. My two favorite vegetables, tomatoes and okra, are good together.

> *Tomatoes and okra* is a nonrestrictive compound appositive. Such compounds are usually set off by commas. For emphasis, a pair of dashes might be used.

3. His three favorite cars — the Edsel, the Studebaker, and the La-Salle — are no longer being manufactured.

Appendix 1

With a nonrestrictive series in the middle of a sentence, a pair of dashes is the only option for setting it off.

4. He lied to three of my friends: Carl, Mary, and Michelle.

4. He lied to three of my friends — Carl, Mary, and Michelle.

Final appositives that are a series may be set off with a colon or a dash.

5. The students talking to Michael, Mary, and Michelle are trying to get them to go to tonight's game.

No colon is needed after a preposition before a series of objects such as these. The present-participle phrase identifies which students, so there is no comma preceding it.

6. While Guy Thibodeaux is eating my two favorite Cajun foods, dirty rice and gumbo, I am watching him with envy.

Here the comma after *gumbo* serves a dual purpose setting off the introductory adverbial clause and enclosing the compound appositive.

Exercise 3

1. Happy that I had won the first set, I continued to rush the net.

The front-shifted adjective phrase should be followed by a comma.

2. My eyes tired from working so long, I closed the book.

The front-shifted nominative absolute should be followed by a comma.

3. My favorite sports — ping pong, basketball, and softball — are not usually dangerous sports.

An appositive not ending with a period and containing a series should be set off by dashes.

4. I like apples, oranges, bananas, and pears.

Nothing is needed before the series of direct objects.

5. I, suspicious of his intent, decided to follow him.

The nonrestrictive adjectival phrase should be set off by commas.

6. My favorite cars, the Lexus and the Infiniti, are comfortable, dependable, and expensive.

For emphasis, dashes could replace the commas around the nonrestrictive compound appositive. The series of adjectives must have commas.

7. I like Fred, the carpenter, and Bill, the electrician.

The appositives giving additional information about Fred and Bill should be set off with commas.

8. My uncle Bob said that he wanted me to have a raise and a vacation and said that he thought that I would get them some year.

No punctuation is needed. *Bob* is in close apposition to *my uncle*. Otherwise, there are just compounds.

9. Although Bob had recommended me for the raise and vacation, I didn't expect them because the big boss, my father-in-law, didn't like me.

Although, a VMCI, introduces a front-shifted verb-modifying clause, so a comma is needed after it. *My father-in-law* is not in close apposition to *the big boss*. So it should be set off with commas.

10. Rex, my orthodontist; Bill, my radiologist; Randy, my general practitioner; and Sue, my podiatrist, pay high liability insurance.

For appositives within a series, semicolons are used to set off the series, and commas set off the appositives.

11. The students eating, drinking, and playing in the mall appear happy.

The present participle phrase identifies which students are being discussed, so no commas set off the phrase.

12. He is studying four subjects: English, algebra, economics, and philosophy.

12. He is studying four subjects — English, algebra, economics, and philosophy.

Either a dashes or a semicolon can be used to begin a series of appositives.

Lesson 5
Exercise 1.
1. I was happy in college, yet I missed my dog.

Yet, a coordinating conjunction here, joins two independent clauses, so a comma is needed.

2. I was happy in college. Nevertheless, I missed my dog.

Nevertheless, a conjunctive adverb, shows the contrastive relationship between two sentences. A comma is needed after it because it is a conjunctive adverb.

3. I was happy in college. But I missed my dog.

   I was happy in college, but I missed my dog.

   But, a coordinating conjunction, shows the contrastive relationship between two sentences or two clauses. No comma is needed after it. It is not a conjunctive adverb.

4. I was happy in college. However, I missed my dog.

   However, a conjunctive adverb, shows the contrastive relationship between two sentences. A comma is needed after it.

5. I was happy in college. I, however, missed my dog.

   However, a conjunctive adverb, shows the contrastive relationship between two sentences. Commas are needed around it.

6. I was happy in college. I missed my dog, however.

   However, a conjunctive adverb, shows the contrastive relationship between two sentences. A comma is needed before it.

7. Though I was happy in college, I missed my dog.

   Though is a VMCI here, so no comma separates it from the clause it introduces. When, as here, the verb-modifying clause is front shifted, a comma follows the clause.

8. I missed my dog though I was happy in college.

   Though is a VMCI here, so no comma separates it from the clause it introduces. When, as here, the clause comes last, no comma is needed.

9. I was happy in college. I missed my dog, though.

   Though, a conjunctive adverb here, shows the contrastive relationship between two sentences. A comma is needed before it.

10. I liked running. Moreover, it was good for me.

    Moreover, a conjunctive adverb, cannot separate two independent with only a comma before it. A semicolon would also be conventional. A comma is needed after *moreover*.

11. I was happy in college. But I missed my dog.

    But, a coordinating conjunction, is not followed by a comma.

12. I was happy in college. But, of course, I missed my dog.

    The pair of commas around *of course* set off the parenthetical. The first one is not there to set off *But*.

Exercise 2

1. I like movies, but I don't like violent movies.

    But, a coordinating conjunction, joins two independent clauses, so a comma is needed before it. A new sentence could begin with *but*. However, a comma would not follow *but*.

2. I worked hard. I, as a result, got a raise.

    As a result is a phrase like the conjunctive adverb *therefore*. It should be set off in commas.

3. I worked hard. As a result, I got a raise.

    As a result is a phrase like the conjunctive adverb *therefore*. It could also have a semicolon preceding it rather than a period. When first, it should be followed by a comma.

4. I worked hard. I got a raise as a result.

    As a result is a phrase like the conjunctive adverb *therefore*. When last in the customary position of an adverbial, it isn't preceded by a comma.

5. I was washing dishes. Mary, meanwhile, was sweeping.

    Meanwhile, a conjunctive adverb, shows the simultaneity of the two sentences. A comma is needed around it.

6. I was washing dishes. Meanwhile, Mary was sweeping.

    Meanwhile, a conjunctive adverb, shows the simultaneity of the two sentences. It could also have a semicolon preceding it rather than a period. A comma is needed after it.

7. I was washing dishes. Mary, at the same time, was sweeping.

    At the same time, a phrase like conjunctive adverb *meanwhile*, shows the simultaneity of the two sentences. A comma is needed around it.

8. I was washing dishes. Mary was sweeping at the same time.

    At the same time is a phrase like the conjunctive adverb *meanwhile*. When last in the customary position of an adverbial, it isn't preceded by a comma.

9. I worked hard. Yet I didn't get a raise.

    Yet, a coordinating conjunction, shows the contrastive relationship between two sentences. No comma is needed after it. It is not a conjunctive adverb.

Exercise 3

1. Unhappily, I can't go to the party.

    Unhappily is an adverbial of attitude modifying the whole sentence. A comma is needed after it.

2. However, I can meet some of you afterwards.

    However, a conjunctive adverb, shows the contrastive relationship between two sentences. A comma is needed after it.

3. But I will be in my work clothes.

    But, a coordinating conjunction, shows the contrastive relationship between two sentences. No comma is needed after it. It is not a conjunctive adverb.

4. Sue, can you meet me?

    Sue is a noun in direct address and should be set off with a comma.

5. Honestly, I can't go.

    Honestly is an adverbial of attitude modifying the whole sentence. A comma is needed after it.

6. I will meet you, instead.

    Instead, a conjunctive adverb, shows the contrastive relationship between two sentences. A comma is needed before it.

7. Well, that's the best I can do.

    Words like *well* probably should not be used in formal writing. If one is used, it should be followed by a comma.

Exercise 4

1. Bob used to work at HEB. But _ he works at Best Buy now.

    But, a coordinating conjunction, shows the contrastive relationship between two sentences. No comma is needed after it. It is not a conjunctive adverb.

2. Bob used to work at HEB. However _ he works at Best Buy now.

    However, a conjunctive adverb, shows the contrastive relationship between two sentences. A comma is needed after it.

3. Susie lost her car key. She has a spare _ though.

    Though, a conjunctive adverb here, shows the contrastive relationship between two sentences. A comma is needed before it. .

4. Though _ Susie lost her car key _ she has a spare.

Though is a VMCI here, so no comma separates it from the clause it introduces. When, as here, the clause is front shifted, a comma follows the clause.

5. Susie lost her car key. She _however _ has a spare.

   However, a conjunctive adverb, shows the contrastive relationship between two sentences. Commas are needed around it.

Lesson 6
Exercise

1. I said she was not reliable.

   Notice that a *that* is understood between *said* and *she*. So this is an indirect quotation, and no comma is needed.

2. I said, "She is not reliable."

   We have a direct quotation here, so a comma and quotation marks are needed. The period always goes inside the quotation marks.

3. I wrote this short apology: "My behavior at the party was abominable."

   The quotation is the same as the apology, so a colon is used. The period always goes inside the quotation marks..

4. Who said, "Life is just a bowl of cherries"?

   The quotation is not a question so the question mark goes outside of the quotation. No period is used inside the quotation marks.

5. Did he say, "Our closest neighbor is Mars"?

   The quotation is not a question, so the question mark goes outside the quotation. No period is used inside the quotation marks.

6. Bill said, "Where are you going tonight?"

   The quotation is a question, so the question mark goes inside the quotation. No period is used at the end.

7. Did Bill say, "Where are you going tonight?"

   Both the main clause and the quotation are questions, so the question mark goes inside the quotation. No period is used at the end.

8. "I want," he said, "a new car."

   The quotation is interrupted, so a comma is used at the point of the interruption and to introduce the second part of the quotation.

9. "I will win the championship," Jim said.
   When the quotation is a direct object and is moved to the front, a comma sets it off.

12. "I don't like Ike" is what we chanted that year.
    I don't like Ike is the subject of the sentence, so it is not separated from the verb by a period or a comma.

13. "Who won?" was what we all asked.
    Who won? is a question, so the question mark is placed inside the quotation mark. The quotation mark is used even though *Who won* is the subject of the sentence.

Lesson 7
Exercise
1. What a nice day!
   Expressions with "what a" require an exclamation mark.

2. I really like flowers.
   Although there is strong feeling being expressed here, an exclamation mark would be inappropriate in formal writing.

3. How nice your new hair style is!
   The exclamatory *how* expression requires an exclamation mark.

4. What was the answer to number one?
   This is not the *what a* exclamation, so no exclamation point should be used.

5. Quit smoking!
   Commands such as this can have different degrees of emphasis. If less, a period could replace the exclamation point.

6. Wow!
   Wow is an exclamatory word which always requires an exclamation mark.

7. He said, "Ouch!"
   The exclamation point goes inside the quotation mark.

Appendix 2

Practice Tests

Practice Test 1

Is a mark of punctuation needed at the place or places underlined. If so, which one? Explain.

1. He wanted me to say what I wanted for Christmas _ but I refused to because I think he should think of something appropriate himself.

2. Although he wanted me to say what I wanted for Christmas _ I refused to because I think he should think of something appropriate himself.

3. He wanted me to say what I wanted for Christmas _ however _ I refused to because I think he should think of something appropriate himself.

4. He wanted me to say what I wanted for Christmas _ I _ however _ refused to because I think he should think of something appropriate himself.

5. He wanted me to say what I wanted for Christmas _ I refused to _ however _ because I think he should think of something appropriate himself.

6. I saved money _ but I don't have enough to go to France yet.

7. I saved money _ yet I don't have enough to go to France.

8. In spite of saving money _ I don't have enough to go to France.

Practice Test 2

Is a mark of punctuation needed at the place or places underlined? If so, which one? Explain.

1. I saved my money _ so I could go to France.

2. I saved my money _ so I was able to buy a car.

3. So I could go to France _ I saved my money.

4. So that I could go to France _ I saved my money.

5. In order for me to go to France _ my mother saved money.

6. I saved my money _ for a trip to France.

7. I was able to buy a car _ for I saved my money.

Practice Test 3

Is a mark of punctuation needed at the place or places underlined? If so, which one? Explain.

1. Mary likes Tom _ and Bill likes Helen.

2. Sue went to the opera _ and the ballet was the choice of Margie.

3. Bill wants an apple _ and Sue wants an orange.

4. Bill will work on his English _ and then he will wash his dog.

5. Bill will work on his English _ and then will wash his dog.

6. He likes history _ English _ and math.

7. His favorite subjects are history _ English _ and math.

8. He is always talking about his favorite subjects _ history _ and math.

9. He is always talking about his favorite subjects _ history _ English _ and math.

10. His favorite subjects _ history, English, and math _ are not difficult for him.

11. I talked to my favorite teacher _ Dr. Martin Shockley.

12. The teacher who influenced me most was _ Dr. Shockley.

13. My aunt Martha talks about _ her children, her nieces, her mother, her husband, and her dog.

14. I like _ Sarah, my sister-in-law _ Tom, my brother-in-law _ Harold my cousin _ and Beth, my other cousin.

15. A man _ who studies rats _ has written a new book about their intelligence.

16. Thomas Gibson _ who does research with rats _ has written a new book about their intelligence.

Practice Test 4

Is a mark of punctuation needed at the place or places underlined? If so, which one? Explain.

1. That he told a lie _ and that he wasn't caught _ may encourage Fred in his deceit.

2. I know that he left early _ and he didn't pick up his mess.

3. When he lies and gets away with it _ I get mad

4. He told an absolute whopper _ and people believed him.

5. I suppose that he will be caught _ that he will be punished _ and that he will learn to tell the truth.

6. I suppose that he will be caught _ he will be punished and _ he will learn to tell the truth.

7. I suppose that he will be caught _ will be punished _ and will learn to tell the truth.

Practice Test 5

Is a mark of punctuation needed at the place or places underlined. If so, which one? Explain.

1. I know that Bob works hard _ and that he should get a promotion.

2. I know that Bob works hard, that he should get a promotion _ and that he should be given a raise.

3. If Tom gets through with his work in time _ Mary can pick him up on the way home.

4. Mary can pick Tom up on the way home _ if he gets through with his work in time.

5. Carla Thomas _ who is a medical doctor _ will not work on my dogs when they are sick.

6. I would pay her _ but she says that if she works on dogs _ she must have different malpractice insurance.

7. A man _ who has a sick dog _ may wish he carried pet-care insurance.

8. I didn't think my dogs would attack a porcupine again _ however _ they did yesterday.

9. My dogs _ two wire-haired dachshunds _ are incredibly stubborn.

10. I own three vehicles _ a 56 Ford tractor, a 1992 F150 truck _ and a 1993 Lexus.

11. My best friends _ Glenn, Jim _ and Tom _ will be at my party.

12. Don _ the offshore diver _ Jim _ the company president _ Tom the engineer _ and Bill _ the radiologist _ are usually late to the party.

13. Bob swept the floor with great care _ and carried the trash to the dumpster.

14. He works hard _ because of his great need for money to feed his kids.

15. Bob used to own _ a Ford, a Chevrolet, an Oldsmobile _ and a Buick

16. Honestly _ Bob forgot _ when to go to his own wedding.

17. Bob walked away from a good job _ because he had to move in order to get married.

Practice Test 6

Is a mark of punctuation needed at the place or places underlined? If so, which one? Explain.

1. Well _ you never can tell.

2. Honestly _ I'm not surprised.

3. He came in _ his arms wrapped in huge bandages.

4. His fingers gripping the bat loosely _ he stroked the ball down the right-field line.

5. Sure that he could beat the throw _ he took off for second on the first pitch.

6. We sat there _ determined not to quit.

7. Frustrated by the inactivity _ Lonnie went into town.

Practice Test 7

Is a mark of punctuation needed at the place or places underlined? If so, which one? Explain.

1. Get out of here _

2. When I tell someone how well I like an idea _ I usually say _ "What a good idea _

3. He said _ "Where did you find that shirt _" _

4. I know how careful he is _

5. How careful you are _

6. Did he say _ "She wants to go to France _ " _

7. Did he say _ that she wants to go to France.

8. Did he ask _ "Are you going to France _ " _

9. Actually _ he asked Marie if she planned a trip to Paris.

10. Frankly _ I think _ he said _ "Whoopee _ " _

11. If he asks _ "What's happening _" _ I say _ "Not much _ " _

12. Bill Walters said _ "We must reduce spending or go out of business _" _

13. "We must reduce spending _ " _ Bill Walters said.

Practice Test 8

Is a mark of punctuation needed at the place or places underlined? If so, which one. Explain..

1. If Bob brings the cake _ and if Susan brings the ice cream, we can celebrate Tom's Birthday.

2. Bob will bring the cake _ and Susan will bring the ice cream.

2. Although Malcolm served well _ and Bruce made few errors, our doubles team lost.

3. If Tom washes dishes _ Bill takes out the trash, and Howie vacuums, we will have a clean house.

4. I said that Tom would wash the dishes _ that Bill would take out the trash, and that Howie would vacuum.

5. Tom will wash the dishes _ Bill will take out the trash, and Howie will vacuum.

6 I said that Tom would wash the dishes _ Bill would take out the trash, and Howie would vacuum.

7. I missed class because Bill forgot to pick me up _ and my car wouldn't run.

8. I think Bill is cleaning the garage _ and Susan is sweeping the deck.

9. I know Bill likes Charlotte _Tom likes Mary, and Hal likes Betty.

Appendix 3

Answers to Practice Tests

Answers to Practice Test 1

1. He wanted me to say what I wanted for Christmas, but I refused to because I think he should think of something appropriate himself.

> A comma is needed to separate independent clauses on each side of *but*, a coordinating conjunction.

2. Although he wanted me to say what I wanted for Christmas, I refused to because I think he should think of something appropriate himself.

> A comma is needed after a front-shifted clause modifying a verb.

3. He wanted me to say what I wanted for Christmas. However, I refused to because I think he should think of something appropriate himself.

> or

3. He wanted me to say what I wanted for Christmas; however, I refused to because I think he should think of something appropriate himself.

> Two independent clauses connected with conjunctive adverb may be separated by a semicolon, but I prefer the more common use of a period and another sentence. A comma before *however* would give you the fault called a comma splice.

4. He wanted me to say what I wanted for Christmas. I, however, refused to because I think he should think of something appropriate himself.

> A conjunctive adverb inside the second clause is conventionally set off by commas.

5. He wanted me to say what I wanted for Christmas. I refused to, however, because I think he should think of something appropriate himself.

> A conjunctive adverb inside the second clause is conventionally set off by commas.

6. I saved money, but I don't have enough to go to France yet.

> A comma is needed to separate independent clauses on each side of *but*, a coordinating conjunction.

7. I saved money, yet I don't have enough to go to France.

   A comma is needed to separate independent clauses on each side of *yet*, a coordinating conjunction.

8. In spite of saving money, I don't have enough to go to France.

   Most often prepositional phrases of contrast are set off by commas. Unless such a phrase is quite long, not using one is not uncommon with good writers.

Practice Test 2

1. I saved my money so I could go to France.

   No comma is needed before *so* when it is a shortened form of *so that*, the VMCI.

2. I saved my money, so I was able to buy a car.

   A comma is needed to separate independent clauses on each side of *yet*, a coordinating conjunction.

3. So I could go to France, I saved my money.

   A comma is needed after a front-shifted clause modifying a verb. This *so* is the shortened form of *so that*, a VMCI.

4. So that I could go to France, I saved my money.

   A comma is needed after a front-shifted clause modifying a verb.

5. In order for me to go to France, my mother saved money.

   A comma is needed after a front-shifted infinitive phrase of motive.

6. I saved my money for a trip to France.

   No comma is needed before a prepositional phrase of motive.

7. I was able to buy a car, for I saved my money.

   A comma is needed to separate independent clauses on each side of *for*, a coordinating conjunction.

Practice Test 3

1. Mary likes Tom, and Bill likes Helen.

   A comma is needed to separate independent clauses on each side of *and*, a coordinating conjunction.

2. Sue went to the opera, and the ballet was the choice of Margie.

    A comma is needed to separate independent clauses on each side of *and*, a coordinating conjunction.

3. Bill wants an apple, and Sue wants an orange.

    A comma is needed to separate independent clauses on each side of *and*, a coordinating conjunction.

4. Bill will work on his English, and then he will wash his dog.

    A comma is needed to separate independent clauses on each side of *and*, a coordinating conjunction.

5. Bill will work on his English and then will wash his dog.

    No comma is needed because compound verb phrases are not separated by a comma.

6. He likes history, English, and chemistry.

    A comma is used before the and because this is a series/

7. His favorite subjects are history, English, and chemistry.

    No mark of punctuation is needed to introduce a series.

8. He is always talking about his favorite subjects, history and math.

    or

8. He is always talking about his favorite subjects: history and math.

or

8. He is always talking about his favorite subjects — history and math.

    Appositives may be set off with a comma when it is not a series. But a colon can be used if the series is followed by a period. A dash can be used to give special emphasis to the appositive.

9. He is always talking about his favorite subject: history, English, and math.

    or

9. He is always talking about his favorite subject — history, English, and math.

    A comma cannot be used to set off the appositive when the appositive is a series.

10. His favorite subjects — history, English, and math — are not difficult for him.

>When the appositive is a series in the middle of the sentence only dashes may be used to set it off.

11. I talked to my favorite teacher, Dr. Martin Shockley.

>A comma is conventional, but a comma or dash may serve to emphasize the appositive more.

12. The teacher who influenced me most was Dr. Shockley.

>No single mark of punctuation should come between a linking verb and a predicate nominal.

13. My aunt Martha talks about her children, her nieces, her mother, her husband, and her dog.

>No single mark of punctuation should come between a preposition and its object—even if the object is a series.

14. I like Sarah, my sister-in-law; Tom, my brother-in-law; Harold, my cousin; and Beth, my other cousin.

>Because commas are needed to separate the appositive from its preceding noun, semicolons must do the job of separating items in the series.

15. Some man who studies rats has written a new book about their intelligence.

>The *who* clause is necessary to identify which man, so no commas are needed.

16. Thomas Gibson, who does research with rats, has written a new book about their intelligence.

>Gibson has been identified, so the *who* clause is parenthetical informations and commas are needed to set it off.

Practice Test 4

1. That he told a lie and that he wasn't caught may encourage Fred in his deceit

>Compound dependent *that* clauses are not separated by commas.

2. I know that he left early and he didn't pick up his mess.

Compound dependent *that* clauses are not separated by commas The second *that* is understood.

3. When he lies and gets away with it, I get mad.

No comma is needed between compound verb, but a comma is needed after the front-shifted clause modifying the verb.

4. He told an absolute whopper, and people believed him.

A comma is needed to separate independent clauses on each side of *and*, a coordinating conjunction.

5. I suppose that he will be caught, that he will be punished, and that he will learn to tell the truth.

Commas are needed for the series.

6. I suppose that he will be caught, he will be punished, and he will learn to tell the truth.

Commas are needed for the series. The last two clauses have *that* understood.

7. I suppose that he will be caught and will be punished

No comma is needed with a compound verb.

Practice Test 5

1. I know that Bob works hard and that he should get a promotion.

Compound dependent *that* clauses are not separated by commas.

2. I know that Bob works hard, that he should get a promotion, and that he should be given a raise.

A comma is needed before the *and* in a series.

3. If Tom gets through with his work in time, Mary can pick him up on the way home.

A comma is needed after a front-shifted clause modifying a verb.

4. Mary can pick Tom up on the way home if he gets through with his work in time.

No comma is needed when the verb modifying clause is in its regular place following the verb.

5. Carla Thomas, who is a medical doctor, will not work on my dogs when they are sick.

Carla Thomas has been identified, so the *who* clause is parenthetical informations and commas are needed to set it off.

6. I would pay her, but she says that if she works on dogs, she must have different malpractice insurance.

A comma is needed before *but* because it separates two independent clause. A comma is needed after the front-shifted clause introduced by *if* even though it's embedded in the *that* clause which is the direct object of *says*.

7. A man who has a sick dog may wish he carried pet-care insurance.

No commas are needed to set off the *who* clause because it identifies which man may wish the insurance.

8. I didn't think my dogs would attack a porcupine again; however, they did yesterday.

A comma is not sufficient to connect two independent clauses introduced by a conjunctive adverb. I prefer replacing the comma with a period and starting a new sentence with *however*.

9. My dogs, two wire-haired dachshunds, are incredibly stubborn.

The *my* identifes the dogs, so the appositive must have commas to set it off.

10. I own three vehicles: a 56 Ford tractor, a 1994 F150 truck, and a 1993 Lexus.

Because the appositive is a series coming at the end, either a colon or a dash could be used to set it off.

11. My best friends — Glenn, Jim, and Tom — will be at my party.

Because the appositive is a series coming in the middle of the sentence, only a pair of dashes can set it off. A comma is needed before the and to complete the series.

12. Don, the offshore diver; Jim, the company president; Tom, the engineer; and Bill, the radiologist, are usually late to the party.

Because commas are needed to separate the appositive from its preceding noun, semicolons must do the job of separating items in the series.

13. Bob swept the floor with great care and carried the trash to the dumpster.

No comma is needed with compound verbs.

14. He works hard because of his great need for money to feed his kids.

   No comma is needed when a prepositional phrase modifying the verb follows it.

15. Bob used to own a Ford, a Chevrolet, an Oldsmobile, and a Buick.

   No punctuation should come between a verb and a direct object unless the direct object is a quotation.

16. Honestly, Bob forgot when to go to his own wedding.

   Honestly is a parenthetical, and a comma is needed to set it off. No comma is needed when the clause modifying the verb follows it.

17. Bob walked away from a good job because he had to move in order to get married.

   No comma is needed when the clause modifying the verb follows it.

Practice Test 6

1. Well, you never can tell.

   The parenthetical *well* should be set off.

2. Honestly, I'm not surprised.

   The adverb of attitude should be set off with a comma.

3. He came in, his arms wrapped in huge bandages.

   Nominative absolutes should be set off by a comma

4. His fingers gripping the bat loosely, he stroked the ball down the right-field line.

   Nominative absolutes should be set off by a comma

5. Sure that he could beat the throw, he took off for second on the first pitch.

   Front-shifted adjective phrases should be set off by a comma.

6. We sat there, determined not to quit.

   End-shifted past-participle phrases should be set off by a comma.

7. Frustrated by the inactivity, Lonnie went into town.

   Front-shifted past-participle phrases should be set off by a comma.

Practice Test 7

1. Get out of here.

    or

1. "Get out of here!"

    Commands such as this can have different degrees of emphasis. If less, a period could replace the exclamation point.

2. When I tell someone how well I like an idea, I usually say, "What a good idea!"

    Exclamation points should be inside the quotation marks. *What a* expressions should be ended with exclamation points.

3. He said, "Where did you find that shirt?"

    A comma is needed to introduce the quote after the verb. The quoted material is the question, so the question mark should be inside the quotation marks.

4. I know how careful he is.

    This is not an emphatic *how* expression, so no exclamation point is used.

5. How careful you are!

    This is an emphatic *how* expression, so an exclamation point is required.

6. Did he say, "She wants to go to France"?

    A comma is needed to introduce the quote after the verb. The quoted material is not the question, so the question mark should be outside the quotation marks.

7. Did he say that she wants to go to France.

    No comma is needed before indirect quotations.

8. Did he ask, "Are you going to France?"

    A comma is needed to introduce the quote after the verb. When the quoted material and the man clause or questions, the question mark should be inside the quotation marks.

9. Actually, he asked Marie if she planned a trip to Paris.

    Actually is a parenthetical and should be set off by a comma.

10. Frankly, I think he said, "Whoopee!"

    Frankly is a parenthetical and should be set off by a comma. A comma is needed to introduce the quote after the verb. Exclamation points should

94 Purposeful Punctuation

be inside the quotation marks. No comma is needed before the dependent clause following *think* . *That* is understood following *think*.

11. If he asks, "What's happening?" I say, "Not much."

    When there is a question mark at the end of a front-shifted verb modifying clause, no comma is needed to set it off.

12. Bill Walters said, "We must reduce spending or go out of business."

    Periods go inside the quotation marks.

13. "We must reduce spending," Bill Walters said.

    Only a comma is needed even though the quoted material is a complete sentence.

Practice Test 8

Is a mark of punctuation needed at the place or places underlined? If so, which one. Explain..

1. If Bob brings the cake _ and if Susan brings the ice cream, we can celebrate Tom's Birthday.

    Two dependent *if* clauses are not separated by a comma.

2. Bob will bring the cake _ and Susan will bring the ice cream

    A comma is needed with the *and* in order to separate two independent clauses.

2. Although Malcolm served well _ and Bruce made few errors, our doubles team lost.

    An *although* is understood before *Bruce*, so the clause beginning with *Bruce* is dependent, so no comma is needed.

3. If Tom washes dishes _ Bill takes out the trash, and Howie vacuums, we will have a clean house.

    A comma is needed because of the series of dependent clauses. *If* is understood before *Bill* and *Howie*.

4. I said that Tom would wash the dishes _ that Bill would take out the trash, and that Howie would vacuum.

    A comma is needed because of the series of dependent clauses.

5. Tom will wash the dishes _ Bill will take out the trash, and Howie will vacuum.

Many writers punctuate a series of independent clauses with a comma between the first and second, but the more conventional usage is to employ a semicolon.

6 I said that Tom would wash the dishes _ Bill would take out the trash, and Howie would vacuum.

A comma is needed because of the series of dependent *that* clauses.

7. I missed class because Bill forgot to pick me up _ and my car wouldn't run.

An understood *because* precedes *my car*, so no comma is needed between two dependent clauses.

8. I think Bill is cleaning the garage _ and Susan is sweeping the deck.

An understood *that* precedes *Bill* and *Susan*, so no comma is needed between two dependent clauses.

9. I know Bill likes Charlotte _Tom likes Mary, and Hal likes Betty.

An understood *that* precedes *Bill, Tom,* and *Hal*, so a comma is needed to separate the second and third dependent clauses in the series.

www.ingramcontent.com/pod-product-compliance
Lightning Source LLC
Chambersburg PA
CBHW081500040426
42446CB00016B/3321